THE FORTS OF NEW FRANCE

The Great Lakes, the Plains and the Gulf Coast
1600–1763

RENÉ CHARTRAND

ILLUSTRATED BY BRIAN DELF

Series editor Marcus Cowper

First published in 2010 by Osprey Publishing
Midland House, West Way, Botley, Oxford OX2 0PH, UK
44–02 23rd St, Suite 219, Long Island City, NY 11101, USA
E-mail: info@ospreypublishing.com

ISBN: 978 1 84603 504 3
E-book ISBN: 978 1 84908 272 3

Editorial by Ilios Publishing Ltd, Oxford, UK (www.iliospublishing.com)
Cartography: Map Studio, Romsey, UK
Page layout by Ken Vail Graphic Design, Cambridge, UK (kvgd.com)
Typeset in Myriad and Sabon
Index by Margaret Vaudrey
Originated by PPS GRasmere, Leeds, UK
Printed in China through Bookbuilders

10 11 12 13 14   10 9 8 7 6 5 4 3 2 1

A CIP catalog record for this book is available from the British Library.

FOR A CATALOG OF ALL BOOKS PUBLISHED BY OSPREY MILITARY AND AVIATION PLEASE CONTACT:

Osprey Direct, c/o Random House Distribution Center, 400 Hahn Road, Westminster, MD 21157
E-mail: uscustomerservice@ospreypublishing.com

Osprey Direct, The Book Service Ltd, Distribution Centre, Colchester Road, Frating Green, Colchester, Essex, CO7 7DW
E-mail: customerservice@ospreypublishing.com

www.ospreypublishing.com

THE FORTRESS STUDY GROUP (FSG)

The object of the FSG is to advance the education of the public in the study of all aspects of fortifications and their armaments, especially works constructed to mount or resist artillery. The FSG holds an annual conference in September over a long weekend with visits and evening lectures, an annual tour abroad lasting about eight days, and an annual Members' Day.

The FSG journal FORT is published annually, and its newsletter Casemate is published three times a year. Membership is international. For further details, please contact:

Website: www.fsgfort.com
Secretary: secretary@fsgfort.com

THE WOODLAND TRUST

Osprey Publishing are supporting the Woodland Trust, the UK's leading woodland conservation charity, by funding the dedication of trees.

ACKNOWLEDGMENTS

The author wishes to acknowledge the very kind assistance of Lyle Cubberly of Illinois, Brian Leigh Dunnigan formerly of forts Michilimackinac and Niagara, Dr. Michael S. Nassaney of Western Michigan University, the staff (amongst whom are many former colleagues) at forts administered by the National Historic Sites of Parks Canada, the staff at Library and Archives Canada in Ottawa, the Archives Nationales (France), the National Archives (UK), the Library of Congress (Washington, DC), the Canadian War Museum (Ottawa), Fort de Chartres State Historic Site, Sainte-Marie among the Hurons (Midland, Ontario).

ARTIST'S NOTE

Readers may care to note that the original paintings from which the color plates in this book were prepared are available for private sale. All reproduction copyright whatsoever is retained by the Publishers. All enquiries should be addressed to:

7 Burcot Park, Burcot, Abingdon, OX14 3DH, UK

The Publishers regret that they can enter into no correspondence upon this matter.

AUTHOR'S NOTE

This work is the second of a two-part series. The first part of this study, Osprey Fortress 75: *The Forts of New France in Northeast America 1600–1763*, concentrated on forts on the Atlantic coast, and on the St Lawrence, Richelieu, Ohio, and Ottawa River valleys. This second part deals with forts of the Great Lakes and the western prairies, the Mississippi Valley and the Gulf of Mexico. These books are a companion to Osprey Fortress 27: *French Fortresses in North America 1535–1763*, which dealt with the fortified cities of Québec, Montréal, Louisbourg and New Orleans. It is hoped that these three lavishly illustrated Osprey Fortress books will form the most important illustrated account yet published of New France's truly extraordinary fortification network.

Unless accompanied by a negative number or otherwise indicated, all photos are by the author.

MEASUREMENTS

Unless otherwise indicated, I have given French feet and inches as they appeared in the 17th and 18th century documentation. It is most important to note that the French foot, used in New France, was not the same as the English foot (still officially used in the USA). The French 12 inches is longer and comes to 12.789 inches in English measurements.

The official French measures from 1668 to 1840 were:

2 miles for 1 *lieue* = 3.898km
1,000 *toises* for 1 mile = 1.949km (English mile = 1.61km)
6 feet for 1 *toise* = 1.949m (English fathom = 1.83m)
12 inches for 1 foot = 32.484cm (English foot = 30.48cm)
12 lines for 1 inch = 2.707cm (English inch = 2.54cm)

CONTENTS

THE FORTS OF NEW FRANCE:
THE GREAT LAKES, THE PLAINS AND THE GULF COAST 1600–1763

INTRODUCTION

The expansion of New France into a vast territory that went from the St Lawrence Valley in Canada forming a great arc that went all the way down to the Gulf of Mexico, and whose western boundaries eventually reached the Rocky Mountains, is a major phenomenon in North American history. It resulted in an amazing network of fortifications, the diversity of which was considerable and evolved over time. The initial early stockade fort might become larger to encompass more housing over the years, such as at Détroit and Michilimackinac, or be rebuilt in stone, such as forts Frontenac or de Chartres. A few, such as Fort Niagara and Fort Condé, featured elaborate fortifications designed to face a European enemy equipped with artillery. Most, however, were designed to face an Indian enemy for whom a wooden fort was generally sufficient. For all the forts mentioned in this book, there were still others whose existence was tenuous and obscure at best. A final remark is that

Canadian fur traders were the catalyst for the extraordinary penetration into the interior of the North American continent. Be they called "voyageurs," *coureurs des bois*, gentlemen, soldiers, or militiamen, they were, in a sense, all of these put together. They sought alliances with Indian nations to trade with and explored ever deeper into the unknown to find new lands where they would set up trade forts that represented their nation. This remarkable life-sized diorama in Pittsburgh's Fort Pitt Museum shows all the essential elements: the canoe full of European goods such as beads, cloth, guns, powder and brandy barrels, metal tools, and utencils that were exchanged for fur pelts. The Canadian summer costume worn was typical of most men on the frontier: a rough linen shirt, a waist sash, breechclouts, "mitasses" (leggings), moccasins, and a cap or bandanna. A hooded "capot" coat was also worn if it was cold.

the hostile Indian nations in the Mississippi Valley also built forts, and ones that incorporated the features of those of their French opponents.

This web of forts had, from the early 18th century, a fairly formal command network, especially after 1717 with the transfer of the Illinois territory to the administrative jurisdiction of Louisiana. The forts of the Great Lakes had the fortress of Quebec City, capital of Canada, as their overall command center. There were three regional command forts: Fort Frontenac oversaw forts Niagara and Toronto; Fort Détroit oversaw forts Saint Joseph, Miamis, Ouiatenon, etc.; and Fort Michilimackinac oversaw forts La Baie, Sault Sainte-Marie, Kaministiquaya, Nipigon, etc., and the western outposts.

The forts of Louisiana had the city of New Orleans, capital of the colony, as their overall command center. Owing to geographical factors, New Orleans was also the regional command center for forts Natchez, Arkansas, Tonicas, Yazous, and Natchitoches. Mobile oversaw fort Toulouse, Tombecbé, etc. Fort de Chartres in Illinois oversaw Kaskasia, Cahokia, Vincennes, etc.

The commandant of a regional center was senior to the other fort commanders even if he held the same rank. The structure was flexible and there could be some groupings or overlapping in some circumstances. And, although attached to Michilimackinac, the western outposts on the Great Plains were essentially a nearly independent sub-command, for reasons of geography and distance.

CHRONOLOGY

1608	Québec founded, becomes the capital of New France.
1620s and 1630s	Exploration of the Great Lakes.
1634	Trois-Rivières founded.
1639	Sainte-Marie among the Hurons founded and then abandoned ten years later.
1642	Montréal founded, becomes business and military hub of Canada's interior territories.
1650s	Exploration of Lake Superior and its watersheds.
1656–58	Sainte-Marie de Gannentaha (among the Iroquois) founded, but abandoned.
1660s and 1670s	Exploration of upper basins of Mississippi River and its linked rivers; Louis Jolliet and Father Marquette descend Mississippi River as far as Arkansas; several missions and trade forts such as Michilimackinac established.
1673	Fort Frontenac established in July on the northern shore of Lake Ontario.
1682	La Salle descends the Mississippi and reaches the Gulf of Mexico. Formally takes possession of the whole area for France and names it Louisiana, after King Louis XIV.
1685–87	La Salle's ill-fated colony at Fort Louis in Texas.
1698	Mission and fort built at Cahokia in Illinois, where other forts and settlements are established in the following decades.

1699	D'Iberville builds Fort Maurepas at Biloxi; more forts and settlements made at Mobile and other sites on the Gulf Coast in the following years.
1701	Fort Détroit founded.
1710s and 1720s	Exploration of Missouri, Osage, Arkansas, Red, Alabama, and Ohio rivers.
1712	Fox Indians fail to take Détroit in May and are defeated in counterattack.
1715	Fort Saint-Jean-Baptiste de Natchitoches built near Spanish Texas border. Fort Michilimackinac and other forts in the western Great Lakes area receive garrisons in the following years.
1716	French troops and allied Indians defeat Fox Indians in August (in Wisconsin).
1717	Illinois (or Upper Louisiana) incorporated administratively to the colony of Louisiana on September 27.
1718–20	War with Spain. Pensacola taken, lost and retaken by the French in 1719.
1722	New Orleans becomes capital of Louisiana.
1728	Large French and allied Indian force attacks the hostile Fox Indians and destroys their towns (in Wisconsin), but most of the Fox escape.
1726	Fort Niagara built to counter the British Fort Oswego built farther east.
1729–30	Natchez Indians take Fort Rosalie (Natchez), a French expedition defeats the Natchez and builds a new fort.
1730	Fox Indians defeated in August and September by French troops and allied Indians from forts Saint Joseph and Miamis.
1735	Last remnants of Fox Indians allied with Sauks defeated in April by French and allied Indians at their Des Moines River fort (Iowa).
1736	Unsuccessful French expeditions against Chickasaw Indians in Louisiana.
1739–40	Louisiana and metropolitan French troops and allied Indians attack Chickasaw Indians, are initially repulsed, but Chickasaws finally sue for peace after another attack from Canadian troops and Indians.
1730s and 1740s	La Vérendrye explores the northern Great Plains west of Lake Superior; builds several small forts on the Prairies. In January 1743, La Vérendrye's sons reach the Rocky Mountains.
1752	Miami Indians, who switched alliances from the French to the British, are defeated and almost annihilated at Pickawillany (Pica, Ohio) by French and allied Indians from Michilimackinac.

Locations of the key sites mentioned in the text

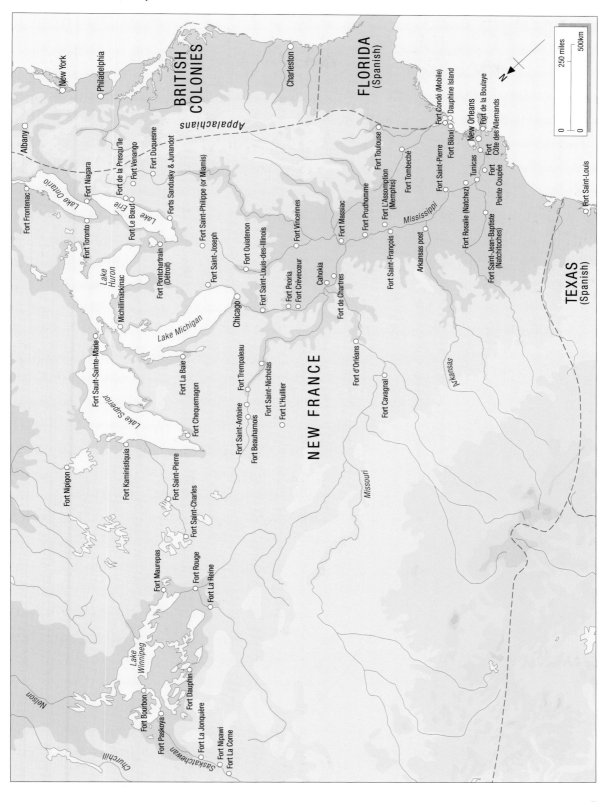

BRITISH COLONIES

New York
Philadelphia
Charleston

FLORIDA (Spanish)

Appalachians

Albany

Fort Frontenac
Fort Niagara
Fort de la Presqu'île
Fort Venango
Fort Duquesne
Forts Sandusky & Junandot

Lake Ontario
Fort Toronto
Fort Le Bœuf
Lake Erie
Forts Saint-Philippe (or Miamis)
Fort Vincennes
Fort Toulouse
Fort Condé (Mobile)
Dauphine Island
Fort Biloxi
New Orleans
Fort de la Boulaye
Côte des Allemands

Lake Huron
Michilimackinac
Fort Pontchartrain (Détroit)
Fort Saint-Joseph
Fort Ouiatenon
Fort Saint-Louis-des-Illinois
Fort Crèvecœur
Fort Peoria
Cahokia
Fort de Chartres
Fort Massiac
Fort Prudhomme
Fort L'Assomption (Memphis)
Fort Tombecbé
Fort Saint-Pierre
Tunicas
Fort
Fort Rosalie (Natchez)
Pointe Coupée
Fort Saint-Jean-Baptiste (Natchitoches)
Fort Saint-François
Arkansas post
Fort Saint-Louis

Lake Superior
Fort Sault-Sainte-Marie
Lake Michigan
Chicago
Fort Trempaleau
Fort Saint-Nicholas
Fort d'Orléans
Mississippi
Arkansas

Fort La Baie
Fort Chequemagon
Fort Saint-Antoine
Fort Beauharnois
Fort L'Huillier
NEW FRANCE
Fort Cavagnal

Fort Nipigon
Fort Kaministiquia
Fort Saint-Pierre
Fort Saint-Charles
Missouri

Fort Maurepas
Fort Rouge
Fort La Reine

TEXAS (Spanish)

Lake Winnipeg
Nelson
Fort Bourbon
Fort Dauphin
Fort La Jonquière
Fort Paskoya
Fort Nipawi
Fort La Corne
Saskatchewan
Churchill

N

250 miles   500km
0
0

7

The fundamental design of Indian fortified towns and early European frontier forts had many common features and both types of fortifications could be difficult to besiege since it was next to impossible to deploy siege artillery in the wilderness. This detail of an engraving after a drawing by Samuel de Champlain shows the 1615 assault on an Iroquois Onondaga village by Champlain, his French companions, and allied Huron Indians. To overcome the stockade, the French, taking a cue from medieval warfare, constructed a cavalier "which commanded them from above their palisades: on which cavalier four or five of our arquebusiers would be placed who should fire down upon their palisades and galleries… Their village was enclosed with four good palisades of large pieces of wood, interlaced with each other, where there was not more than a half-foot between them, thirty feet (9m) high, and the galleries as in the manner of a parapet that they covered with double pieces of wood" according to Champlain. European frontier forts rarely had such elaborate defenses. (Library and Archives Canada, C5749)

1756	British Oswego, New York, taken by French in September.
1758	Fort Frontenac taken in August by an Anglo-American force on a daring raid; the fort is abandoned.
1759	Fort Niagara taken in July by an Anglo-American army. Québec falls to the British in September.
1760	French army in Canada surrenders at Montréal in September. French garrisons in the Great Lakes replaced by British troops in the following years.
1762	French reinforcements arrive in New Orleans.
1763	By the Treaty of Paris, France cedes Canada and land up to the east bank of the Mississippi River to Great Britain, and land from the west bank of the Mississippi to Spain.
1764–69	French garrisons in Louisiana much reduced and gradually replaced by British and Spanish troops.

THE EARLY FORTS OF THE GREAT LAKES

From the earliest days of the French settlement at Québec, the call of the wilderness was overwhelming. Samuel de Champlain, Québec's founder and first governor was an avid explorer and cartographer. Many others followed his footsteps. One can cite Étienne Brulé (1592–1633) in particular. He was a young clerk at Québec who learned Indian languages, became a translator and chose to live and trade with the Indians. The extent of his travels are still not clear because he did not leave a record of his voyages into the interior; they are known by the early accounts of those who knew him. He is credited with probably being the first European to see four of the five Great Lakes (his route did not go past Lake Michigan). This large area was often called "Les pays d'en Haut" (the "Upper Country"). Brûlé also headed south to what is now Pennsylvania

and there is speculation that he may have even reached Chesapeake Bay. Criticized by missionaries for his freewheeling lifestyle amongst the Indians, his example was contagious to other young Frenchmen who soon sought a free if risky life in the wilderness. The Indians and the early *coureurs des bois* were content to travel to Québec to trade. Only in 1634 was a second post established at Trois-Rivières on the St Lawrence River.

French missionaries took the next step. Their evangelical zeal to spread the word of God to the Indian nations brought them ever deeper into the continent's interior. By the 1620s, they frequented the large and powerful Huron nation on the northeastern shores of Lake Huron, some 800 miles (1300km) west of Québec. By the mid-1630s, religious authorities felt they had to have a permanent base there. From 1639, the Jesuit missionaries established a substantial fortified mission in the center of the Huron's domain, which they called Sainte-Marie among the Hurons, from which several other missions were established nearby.

Meanwhile, Montréal had been founded in 1642 by a group of devout French settlers who called it Ville-Marie (City of Mary). Business and military interests soon overtook religious concerns due to Montréal's exceptional strategic location. From Montréal, the Great Lakes could be reached by the western St Lawrence River, which led to Lake Ontario and Erie, and by the Ottawa River, which led to Lake Huron and from thence to lakes Huron, Michigan, and Superior.

The Jesuit missions on Lake Huron expanded during the 1640s thanks to the fur trade amongst friendly Indians. Sainte-Marie, the HQ mission, was a remarkably well-fortified compound featuring stone structures as well as stockades. A few soldiers were also attached to this fort. By 1648, there were over 60 Frenchmen there, which represented a fifth of the colony's small population. However, the missions were doomed. Successive epidemics of smallpox had killed well over half of the once-powerful Huron nation, and its ancient Iroquois enemy, less affected by epidemics, mounted a general attack. Some adjacent missions fell and, in 1649, fearing an assault, Sainte-Marie's residents abandoned the mission, which they burned as they left, and took refuge in a new fort they built on Christian's Island. Lack of provisions brought great hardships during the following winter, and, in June 1650, the French, accompanied by about 300 Christian Hurons, left for Québec.

Apart from temporary fur-trading posts, no substantial new forts were established in the following

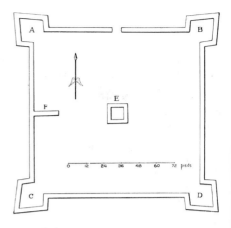

Plan of the second Fort Sainte-Marie among the Hurons, 1649–50. Situated on Christian's Island, this fort of about 100ft² (9.8m²) had a regular plan compared with the irregular layout of the previous fort and was thus easier to defend. The letters A, B, C, and D indicate bastions, E is the site of a masonry cistern, and F may have been part of a secondary wall. It was made with stone and mortar and its walls were 14ft (4.5m) high according to Father Raguneau. During the dreadful winter of 1649–50, it contained over 100 dwellings that housed about 6,000 Hurons, dying from starvation and disease. (Print after the plan of an 1855 survey made by Father F. Martin. Private collection)

A Jesuit missionary priest, *c.*1700. Missionaries were important in the explorations and wilderness forts of New France, both in Canada and Louisiana. Jesuit priests wearing their "Black Robes" were predominant in Canada from the 1630s and, although some of their early missions failed, they persisted. By the 18th century, most of the major forts on the Great Lakes and Louisiana had a Jesuit missionary that was also the garrison's chaplain. There were some 16 Jesuits in Canada and ten in Louisiana in the mid-18th century. The Jesuit superior residing at Michilimackinac was the delegate of the bishop of New France for the "Upper Country" as was the superior in New Orleans for Louisiana. (Contemporary print. Private collection)

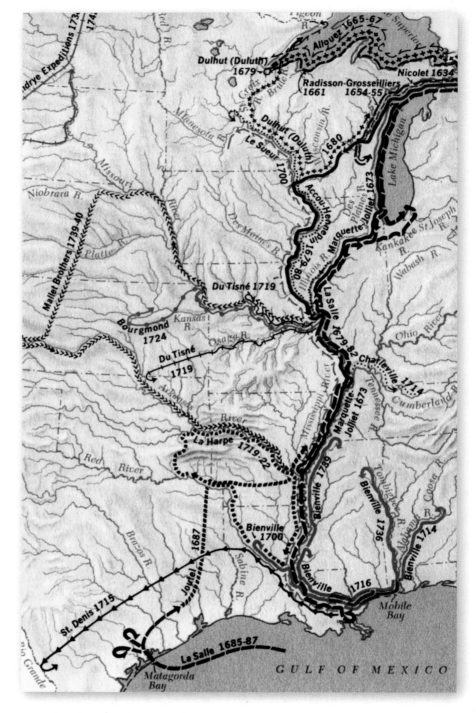

Routes of French explorers in the western Great Lakes, the Mississippi Valley, the Great Plains, and the Gulf Coast, within the present United States of America. (US National Park Service)

years by the French except for the short-lived Sainte-Marie de Gannentaha (several spellings used, now known as Sainte-Marie amongst the Iroquois) just below Lake Ontario. During negotiations between the French and the Onondaga nation of the Iroquois Confederacy during 1654 and 1655, the Onondaga chiefs invited the French to be their friends and allies and build a fort with missionaries and soldiers on their territory south of Lake Ontario. In response to the Onondaga's invitation, the French opted to establish a

fortified and garrisoned mission. On May 17 1656, a large flotilla of canoes left Québec led by Zacharie Dupuis, the former commandant of Québec's garrison, with over 40 soldiers and workmen, seven Jesuit priests and many Indians. In the lead canoe flew the white silk standard of France with the word "JESUS" painted thereon. On July 11, the party landed on the shores of Lake Gannentaha (now Lake Oneida at Syracuse, New York), fired their guns in a "feu de joie" and, six days later, got to work building the mission-fort. In August 1657, three settlers were killed near Montréal. The newly appointed Governor d'Ailleboust had no experience of Indian diplomacy, suspected the Mohawk nation of the Iroquois to be responsible and ordered all Mohawks in the French settlements arrested. In retaliation, it was rumored that the Mohawks would attack Fort Sainte-Marie de Gannentaha. The 40 or so Frenchmen in the fort were not reassured as they felt themselves to be "in the midst of our enemy" as Pierre Radisson put it. Since the arrival of the French, an epidemic had raged amongst the Onondagas that had caused the death of

The eastern side of Sainte-Marie among the Hurons, 1640s. This reconstruction shows the massive appearance of the large stone bastions between the daunting curtain wall enclosing the European compound of this fortified and garrisoned mission fort.

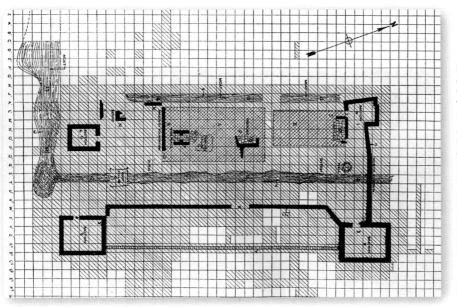

Excavation plan of the mission and fort of Sainte-Marie among the Hurons built from 1639. This plan concerns the European compound. Archaeological excavations in the 1940s revealed substantial fortifications featuring large masonry tower-like bastions and some stone curtain walls on the north and east sides. Stockade walls edged wet moats on the south and west sides. A narrow canal, suitable for canoes, also went through the fort. This plan was made in 1949. (Sainte-Marie among the Hurons, Ontario Ministry of Tourism, Midland, Ontario)

up to 500 children besides a number of adults. Yet the Onondagas did not wish to attack the French fort. It turned out that Oneida Iroquois warriors had killed the three settlers, but the Mohawk Iroquois remained outraged at the French. Overtaken by fear, the French in Sainte-Marie de Gannentaha abandoned the fort on March 20, 1658, furtively sneaking out of the area.

In April 1658, Oneida ambassadors arrived at Québec to admit their responsibility in the killing of the three Frenchmen and to negotiate the release of Mohawk hostages. They also carried a message from the Onondagas stating "it is thou, Frenchman, that has broken the bond [of friendship] by departing from my country without my knowledge." Nevertheless the Onondagas wished to "renew friendship … more strongly than ever" and preserved the "house at Gannentaha; thy lodgings are still standing… Put thy canoe in the water, and go take possession of what belongs to thee." And indeed, as late as 1669 when Father Frémin visited the abandoned fort, he reported it to be in the same condition as when he had left it 11 years earlier. But the French never came back. It was a major error in the French's diplomacy towards the Iroquois Confederacy that put a shadow on France's western expansion by way of Lake Ontario for the next half-century.

Royal government and frontier forts

In the following years, relations with the Iroquois deteriorated to the point that some in France started to wonder if the settlements in Canada might not be overrun. Furthermore, any expansion westward for the fur trade was next to impossible. The young King Louis XIV was not about to have his overseas subjects massacred by "the barbarous nation of the Iroquois" as he put it in his memoirs and, in 1665, sent some 1,300 troops to Canada to beat back the Iroquois and create new settlements. French territories in North America now came under direct royal administration. New forts were built on the Richelieu River (see Fortress 75: *The Forts of New France in Northeast America 1600–1763*, René Chartrand, Osprey, Oxford, 2008), peace was signed with the Iroquois in 1667, and thousands of new settlers arrived in the St Lawrence Valley. A new wave of explorers set out to chart the continent's interior. By 1673, Louis Jolliet and Father Marquette had descended the Mississippi River as far as Arkansas and Robert Cavelier de La Salle had explored the southern shore of Lake Ontario and part of the Ohio River.

There now came as governor general of New France an energetic man of vision: Louis de Buade, Count of Frontenac, an aristocratic veteran of many European campaigns who took his new posting at Québec in 1672. He was an autocrat and even the king had to intervene when it was learned that he used soldiers of his bodyguard as his own personal police. Frontenac was also a man with a vision and he wrote to Jean-Baptiste Colbert, the powerful minister of Louis XIVs court, that Québec "could not be better located to become one day the capital of a great empire" (C11A, 3). He supported

Cannon barrel found on the site of the second Fort Sainte-Marie among the Hurons on Christian's Island (near Penetanguishene, Ontario) in 1919. It is a 34in. long, wrought iron piece of ordnance with a 4in. bore. It appears that it never had the opportunity to be fired in anger and seems to have been buried when the French and Hurons evacuated the fort in 1650. (Sainte-Marie among the Hurons, Ontario Ministry of Tourism, Midland, Ontario)

explorers and, in July 1673, at the head of a large party, Count Frontenac traveled to Cataraqui, on the northeast shore of Lake Ontario, met Indian leaders with suitable pomp and circumstance and had a large stockade fort built there that became known as Fort Frontenac (now Kingston, Ontario). It was the first fort on the Great Lakes established by the royal government. It was intended to play a leading role in the fur trade, but its ultimate purpose was to exert French influence on the lakes and provide protection and encouragement to traders, explorers, and missionaries.

More stockade frontier forts were built in the following years as far as the upper Mississippi Valley. However, renewed warfare with the Iroquois in the 1680s and 1690s resulted in the withdrawal of the small garrisons in those distant forts, although many French traders stayed in those areas. Starting with the settlement of Détroit in 1701, the same year as the "Great Peace" between the French and many Indian nations (including the Iroquois who had been defeated in the 1690s), royal officers and troops gradually

Reconstruction of the fort and mission of Sainte-Marie de Gannentaha (or among the Iroquois), 1656–58. On July 17, 1656, according to Father d'Ablon, the French missionaries "set to work in good earnest to build lodgings for ourselves, and a good redoubt for the soldiers" on the shores of Lake Onondaga (visible in the background), south of Lake Ontario. There is a bastion at the southwest (right of the image) and another at the northwest (not visible). This reconstruction is Fort Sainte-Marie among the Iroquois Living History Museum at Syracuse, NY.

Interior of the reconstructed fort and mission of Sainte-Marie de Gannentaha (or among the Iroquois), 1656–58. The chapel is at the center, with lodgings and utility buildings on either side. This layout was typical of the early missionary forts. Explorer and fur trader Pierre Esprit Radisson visited the fort in August 1657 and described it as "a most faire castle very neatly built with great trees and well tied in the top with twigs of ashure, strengthened with two strong walles and two bastions, which made the place impregnable." This view is taken from the southwest bastion of Fort Sainte-Marie among the Iroquois Living History Museum, Syracuse, NY.

A SMALL OUTPOST FRONTIER FORT

For many forts built in the wilderness, the records of their appearance are very sketchy, when they exist at all. From what descriptions there are, they could vary in size, a few being fairly large, but most were apparently rather small. While a few had only two bastions, for instance Fort Beauharnois or the first Fort de Chartres, most appear to have had four bastions, the size of which could also vary. The stockade could be a single or a double row of logs. The essential buildings within were quarters for the commandant and the garrison, a storehouse (this could be a single building or several), a guardhouse, and a powder magazine (usually placed in a bastion). Such a fort is illustrated. Some, such as Fort Puskoya, could be even smaller. They were always made of wood except for fireplaces and chimneys. Life in these forts could be lonely and occasionally very dangerous for the men posted there; such small forts could not resist a determined Indian attack for long. Yet these humble forts proved quite effective in fostering the extraordinary French expansion into vast areas of North America.

came back to forts on the shores of the Great Lakes in the next decades. There was some opposition from the Fox Indians, but they were practically annihilated by the 1730s and, by then, French forts were established at all the lakes and farther west as well as down along the Mississippi. Throughout the French regime, the frontier forts of New France also operated as trade centers under a complicated system of monopolies and permits paid by traders to the commandants representing central authority. The forts were absolutely necessary to maintain the trade network, as were their small military garrisons to ensure security and national prestige at the very edge of what was seen as the civilized world.

Lake Ontario

The first Fort Frontenac built in July 1673 was described by Count Frontenac as "having two sides of buildings each forty-six feet long and a store twenty feet

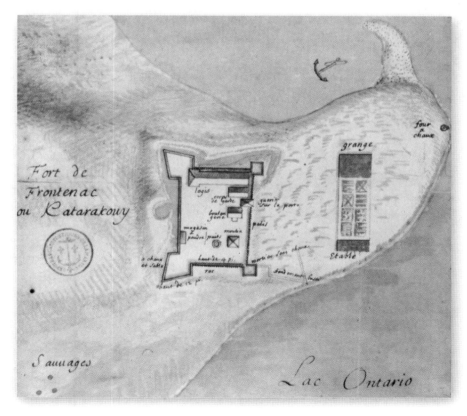

Plan of Fort Frontenac, 1685. Even 14 years after its foundation the fort was still not finished, but Robert Cavelier de La Salle made many improvements when he commanded it: 12ft-high (3.9m) masonry walls and bastions started in 1675 are completed on the landward side, but the lake's side has only small wooden temporary bastions and three curtain walls are still made of logs. A large rectangular building (top) was the lodging, next to a guardhouse, a *guérite* over the gate, a bakery, a mill, a round well, and a powder magazine next to the landward wall. A moat edges the west and north sides. Outside is a garden between a barn and a stable near the lake. Some Indian lodges are noted at lower left. This fort was evacuated in 1689. (Archives Nationales (Aix-en-Provence, France), Dépôt des Fortifications des Colonies, Canada)

long" containing a garrison of 30 men with settlers within its stockade walls. Initially called Fort Cataraqui, it was usually known by its founder's name. This fort was 400ft (130m) around, made of earth supported by a strong palisade. Not only was it a military base, but it was also intended to be a naval base. Several large "barks" that could sail or be rowed on the lake were immediately built there. In 1675, the fort was leased to Robert Cavelier de La Salle on the condition that he improved it and kept it garrisoned. In return, the enterprising La Salle would finance his explorations into the continent's interior thanks to the trade from this and other forts built later. Soon after he took control of the fort, La Salle had the first wooden fort demolished and laid out a much larger masonry fort of 800m around on a square plan with four bastions. By 1682, it was said that "three quarters of" Fort Frontenac was "of masonry of hard stone, the walls" being "three feet thick and twelve high" although it was not completed, one place being only 4ft (1.3m) in height and the remainder being "closed in with stakes." Around was a ditch 15ft (5m) wide. Within was "a house of squared logs, a hundred feet long … a blacksmith's shop, a guardhouse, a house for officers, a well, and a cow-house." Near the fort were "several French houses, an Iroquois village, a convent and a Récollet church." With renewed war against the Iroquois during the 1680s, it was feared that the fort would be overrun. A garrison of 56 soldiers was sent there in 1684 and evacuated in July 1689. Count Frontenac, who came back to Canada for a second term as governor general shortly thereafter, was outraged that "his" fort had been abandoned and, once he had the advantage against the Iroquois, he had the fort reoccupied in 1695 and used it as a base for his successful expedition destroying enemy towns and crops the following year.

The fort's masonry walls still stood and were repaired while new buildings went up in and around the fort. Its military importance decreased as time passed and other forts were built farther west. However, from its shipyard were launched the small sailing vessels that kept communications and

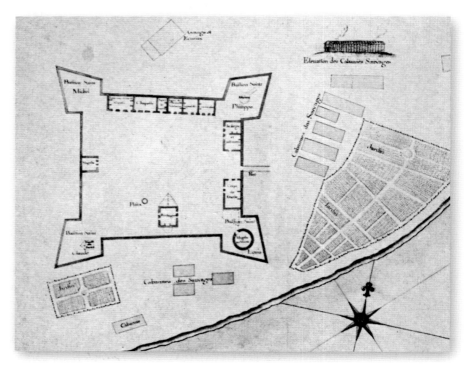

Plan of Fort Frontenac, 1740. Reoccupied and finished in stone from 1695, the bastions and curtain walls are completed on the lake's side. The powder magazine was rebuilt as a round structure made of stone within the southeast bastion. The moat has disappeared. Outside the fort, on the east and south sides, are shown the Indians' longhouses and the gardens. The barn and stable for horses is now on the north side. In 1752, John Defever described Fort Frontenac as being made "of stone, rather larger than at Niagara, [it] has six cannons mounted, the walls extremely decay'd and weak. Here are two officers and between forty and fifty men" in garrison. (Library and Archives Canada)

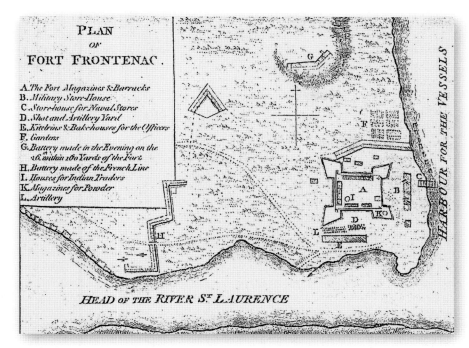

PLAN
OF
FORT FRONTENAC.

A. *The Fort Magazines & Barracks*
B. *Military Store-House*
C. *Storehouse for Naval Stores*
D. *Shot and Artillery Yard*
E. *Kitchins & Bake-houses for the Officers*
F. *Gardens*
G. *Battery made in the Evening on the 26. within 160 Yards of the Fort*
H. *Battery made of the French Line*
I. *Houses for Indian Traders*
K. *Magazines for Powder*
L. *Artillery*

HARBOUR FOR THE VESSELS

HEAD OF THE RIVER St LAURENCE

Plan of Fort Frontenac, 1758. This British plan shows the field fortifications (H, G) made by Lt. Col. Bradstreet's besieging troops in August 1758. The northwest (Saint-Michel) and southwest (Saint-Claude) bastions have been rebuilt to be slightly larger. However, by 1758, the fort was mainly used as a supply depot and could not resist a siege by a sizable European enemy force equipped with artillery. The French garrison built a line between the garden (F) and the fort extending to the lake's shore on the north side, and set up some guns (L) between the southeast bastion and the officers' kitchen and bakehouse (E). (Period printed map. Private collection)

supplies moving with Niagara and Toronto, so it remained an important naval base and supply depot between Montréal and lakes Ontario and Erie. There was no major attack on Fort Frontenac until July 25, 1758 when a large Anglo-American force of about 3,000 men under Lieutenant Colonel Bradstreet landed near the fort, which had only 54 regular officers and men and a few militiamen, all of whom amounted to 110 souls with wives and children. The garrison nevertheless put up some resistance that forced the Anglo-Americans to build siege batteries, but it was hopeless to resist for long and, on July 28, Fort Frontenac surrendered. The Anglo-Americans destroyed part of the fort and the ships in the harbor and then left. The French did not reoccupy it.

Remains of Fort Frontenac. These masonry foundations are those of the southeast (Saint-Louis) bastion, which featured the round powder magazine in the 18th century. These remnants can be seen in the parking lot of the Canadian Forces War College at Canadian Forces Base Fort Frontenac, Kingston, Ontario.

The large stone house built at Fort Niagara from 1726–27. It became known as the "French Castle" and is the first sizeable stone structure built in western New York State. As can be seen in this 2008 photo showing its side facing the fort's interior, its present appearance remains close to the early plans. Old Fort Niagara, Youngstown, NY.

The Niagara River connecting Lake Ontario to Lake Erie was of great strategic importance. In spite of the great Niagara Falls that made navigation on the river impossible, it was the best place to travel from one lake to the other. As they ventured farther west, the French realized the value of this vital link and sought to occupy the area. However, this was the domain of the powerful Iroquois nations established to the south. Nevertheless, Robert Cavelier de La Salle sought to trade with the Indians as well as to explore the continent's interior and, in early 1679, had a small fortified trading post built on a height overlooking the south side of the Lake Ontario entrance to the Niagara River. This fort, named Fort Conti, consisted of two 42ft^2 (4m^2) redoubts made of logs laid horizontally connected by a stockade. It was destroyed by an accidental fire in late 1679 and was not rebuilt.

The *Griffon*, the first full-sized ship to sail on the Great Lakes, 1679. The *Griffon* was a barque 18m long and 4.8m wide with two masts weighing about 45 tons. It was built on Lake Erie near Fort Rémi at Cuyaga Creek (NY), a tributary of the Niagara River several miles from Niagara Falls. Launched on August 7, 1679, the ship was loaded with a cargo of trade goods and, with La Salle and De Tonti on board, sailed west, went up the St Claire River into Lake Huron, crossed the Mackinac Straits into Lake Michigan and arrived at present-day Green Bay to load furs accumulated there. Robert Cavelier de La Salle and Henri De Tonti stayed at Green Bay and, on September 18, the *Griffon* sailed back. It was never heard of again, probably a victim of one of the terrible storms of the Great Lakes that have claimed countless vessels and lives since then. (Print after G. A. Tomlinson. Private collection)

La Salle had meanwhile moved west along the Niagara River to connect with Lake Erie. At about 4 miles (6.4km) above the falls, near a creek on the east shore of the river, he built Fort Rémi (Cayuga Creek, NY). This small post was more like a shipyard. During the spring and summer of 1679, La Salle and his men built the *Griffon*, the first ship to sail on the Great Lakes. In August and September, the *Griffon* traveled on lakes Erie, Huron and Michigan, and then vanished, never to be seen again. It was probably a victim of one the Great Lakes' ferocious storms that have claimed countless ships since. This was not the end of French navigation on the Great Lakes, however. As early as 1687, the French had three small sailing vessels providing transport on that lake in addition to 198 bateaux and 142 canoes, all based at Fort Frontenac. From 1726, two small schooners provided a service between forts Frontenac and Niagara. By 1741, there were four sailing vessels and, during the 1750s, many more. French naval dominance over Lake Ontario was total, until the Seven Years War when the Anglo-Americans started building sailing ships at Oswego. In 1758, Colonel John Bradsteet's successful raid on Fort Frontenac resulted in the destruction or capture of nine armed sloops, which was a fatal blow to French naval power on Lake Ontario. However, the other lakes remained totally under French naval control until the capitulation of Canada in September 1760.

The next fort erected on the shores of Lake Ontario at Niagara was Fort Denonville built in late July 1687. It consisted of a square stockade with four

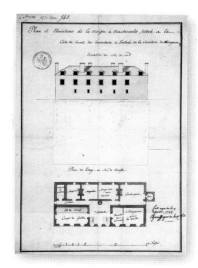

ABOVE
Plan of the "House with *machicoulis*" at Fort Niagara, 1738, by Engineer Lt. Chaussegros de Léry. It is nearly identical to plans made in 1726 and 1727. The elevation shows the northern side facing Lake Ontario. This side is at the top of the ground-floor plan shown below, with five narrow gun ports serving as windows. At left, with thicker walls, were a small powder magazine, three small storerooms, and a bakery. A corridor separated these rooms from, at left, a guardroom, the entrance with stairways, and, at right, a trading store. In 1752 John Defever described the fort as being of "stone about sixteen rods square, the walls about ten feet high, old and decay'd, has six cannons, or embrasures for them, the cannon not being mounted, has two officers and thirty five men" as its garrison. (Archives Nationales, Dépot des Fortifications des Colonies, Canada)

LEFT
Fort Niagara, 1756–57. Plan by Capt. Pierre Pouchot showing the Vauban-style outworks added to the fort from January 1756. Old Fort Niagara, Youngstown, NY.

bastions and was meant to control the Iroquois to the south, but it was not strong enough and its garrison evacuated in September 1688. Following the end of the War of Spanish Succession in 1713 and peace with the Iroquois, French traders were again roaming on the southwestern end of Lake Ontario and, in 1720, a small trading post was built at the foot of the Niagara escarpment with permission of the Seneca nation of the Iroquois (now Artpark in Lewiston, New York).

By the 1720s, the Anglo-Americans were also interested in having a base on Lake Ontario and, in 1722, built a trading post that would become Fort Oswego. It was situated at the mouth of the East River, at the southeastern part of the lake (now Oswego, New York) and was the first non-French establishment built on the Great Lakes. To contain the English and prevent them from penetrating any farther, French agents obtained the land where Fort Denonville had stood from the Senecas to build a new "House of Peace" to trade. Fort Niagara was thus built during 1726–27 and it followed the usual plan of a square stockade with four bastions. What was built inside, however, was radically different than what was found in fur trade forts. Engineer Lieutenant Gaspard-Joseph Chaussegros de Léry designed a large three-story-high stone "fireproof machicolated house" containing a storeroom, quarters for a garrison of about 60 officers and men, a bakery, a magazine, a chapel, and even a well (C11A, 48). It was really a large fortified redoubt. Over the next decades, the stockade was often repaired and expanded with new log buildings built such as barracks and storehouses within. In 1744 the stockade was rebuilt on a larger rectangular plan.

While formidable against an Indian enemy, Fort Niagara was helpless against even a modest Anglo-American force equipped with artillery. All agreed with Captain Malartic that its stockade "looked more like a fence than a fort" (Guerre, A1, 3405). In the fall of 1755, Captain Pierre Pouchot of the Béarn infantry regiment, who had engineering talents, arrived with a detachment of troops with instructions to render the fort tenable against enemy artillery. From late October 1755 until mid-October 1757,

Fort Niagara's new gate with a drawbridge, christened "La porte des Cinq Nations" (The Gate of the Five Nations) in honor of the Iroquois Confederacy was built in 1756. Old Fort Niagara, Youngstown, NY.

new buildings and Vauban-style half-bastions, ravelins and dry ditches were built, and totally enclosed Fort Niagara. A new stone gate with a drawbridge, christened "La porte des Cinq Nations" (The Gate of the Five Nations) in honor of the Iroquois Confederacy, was built in 1756. The following year, a large stone powder magazine was constructed. In 1759, Niagara had less than 500 men in garrison when an Anglo-American army of some 3,000 men under Brigadier General John Prideaux accompanied by 1,000 Iroquois warriors besieged the fort from July 6. Facing such elaborate defenses required formal European-style siege operations especially as Capt. Pouchot conducted a vigorous defense. On July 20, Brig. Prideaux was accidentally killed in one of his mortar batteries and command passed on to Sir William Johnson. On July 24, a French relief force was crushed at La Belle Famille, 2 miles (3.2 km) south of Fort Niagara and the now totally isolated fort surrendered two days later.

Access from Fort Niagara to and from Lake Erie was made by the Niagara River. A portage trail on the east shore was necessary to bypass the formidable and famous Niagara Falls. About 1½ miles (2.4 km) above the falls was a landing for boats and canoes to continue onto Lake Erie. In 1751, a "Fort Petit Niagara" (Fort Small Niagara) was built there to secure the area. It was a "wooden fort, [with] lodgings, [and] a storehouse for conducting the brandy trade that is done there" according to the Chevalier de Raymond. By 1758, another small post had been established at "Petit Rapide" (Little Rapids) where Lake Erie flowed into the Niagara River. Both posts were abandoned in 1759 when the Anglo-American army arrived in the area.

View of Fort Rouillé, also called Fort Toronto, 1750s. This evocative illustration made in the early 20th century by F. S. Challener gives an idea of the fort's exterior appearance: a small stockade fort with a bastion at each corner. According to John Defever, who was taken there in 1752, Toronto was "only a small fort, walled with thick plank, there being no picketts near, they have their plank from Canada. Here is only one officer and ten men" in garrison. It was armed with four small cannons. This site has since spawned into Canada's largest city. The uniforms of the French shown trading with the Indians are not accurate. (Private collection)

Fort Niagara, 1756: Vauban in the wilderness

B

The area of the present city of Toronto was first occupied by the French in 1720 when fur traders built a small trading post near the present Old Mills. Thirty years later, Governor General de La Jonquière felt that a more substantial outpost should be built there and held by a small garrison to secure definitively the northwestern shore of Lake Ontario. It would also intercept trade by Indians of that area to the Anglo-American Fort Oswego. The fort, built at the mouth of the Humber River, was named Fort Rouillé in honor of Antoine-Louis Rouillé, count de Jouy, minister of the navy and colonies in Louis XV's cabinet at the time the fort was constructed. However, everyone knew the area by its Indian name of Toronto and the fort appears to have usually been called Fort Toronto. It consisted of a small palisade fort built on a square plan with a bastion at each of its four corners, and with five buildings inside: a guardhouse, a storeroom, a barracks, a blacksmith's shop, and a residence for the officers. There were no hostile actions at Fort Toronto. Its garrison of 15 soldiers led by Captain Alexandre Douville withdrew after the fall of Niagara in July 1759, burning the fort as they departed. Built on a low bluff, the fort's site was later partly washed away by the lake's erosion and, in 1878–79, it was built over when the Canadian National Exhibition grounds were constructed.

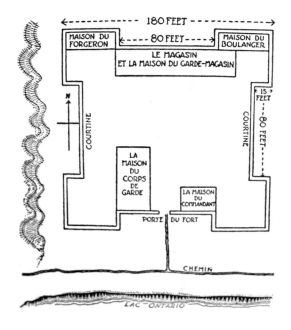

Plan of Fort Rouillé, often called Fort Toronto, 1750–59. It had the usual square plan with four bastions. The bastions on the north side (top) had the lodgings of the blacksmith (left) and of the baker (right). In between was the storehouse with the lodgings of the storekeeper. On the south side facing Lake Ontario (bottom), at either side of the gate stood the guardhouse (left) and the commandant's house (right). (Print after C. W. Jefferys. Private collection)

Lakes Huron and Erie

Part of the Canadian 18th-century fur trade passed onto Lake Huron at Sault Sainte-Marie, the channel and portages of which connected lakes Huron and Superior. A fortified mission was built there by Father Marquette in 1668, but abandoned in 1689. Although Sault Sainte-Marie had been constantly frequented by French missionaries and traders since the late 17th century, it did not have permanent military structures or a military garrison until

---

B FORT NIAGARA, 1756: VAUBAN IN THE WILDERNESS

At the beginning of the Seven Years War, Fort Niagara was deemed totally incapable of resisting a land attack by a British and American force, and it was resolved to render this most important post more defensible. Since it was situated on a point, Capt. Pierre Pouchot enclosed the east side of the fort with two half-bastions connected by a curtain wall protected by ravelins and glacis. The most pressing work was to have the new fortifications completed, and that was done by October 1756. These new earthworks were faced with sods of earth. It was an impressive demonstration of Marshal Vauban's fortification principles in the wilderness of North America and Niagara was the only place on the French frontier where they were extensively applied.

This plate shows the extent of the work between January 14 and October 1756 based on a 1756 plan. The stockades of the old 1726 fort are visible, but these gradually vanished as more quarters were built, notably the two long outer buildings on the north and south sides. To the southwest, a long, new barrack

building faced the Niagara River, while a long storehouse and a new guardhouse faced the new, stone "Gate of the Five Nations" at the southern half-bastion. The grounds of the fort still had the long gully that served as both a convenient drainage brook and a useful natural defense. On the waterfront below the fort was a landing for the vessels, with various installations such as docks and service buildings.

Work at Niagara went on thereafter with more buildings being added, notably behind the east curtain wall. The southwest long barrack was replaced by a smaller storehouse and a stone magazine in 1757, and the gully was filled and transformed into a narrow drainage canal. The fort's main features were not seriously damaged by bombardments in 1759 and 1812–13. The main visual change occurred between 1863 and 1872 when the US Army solidified and improved the old French lines by the addition of a concrete revetment wall, faced with red brick and containing casemated artillery galleries.

Four sailing ships of the French fleet on Lake Ontario, 1757. From 1680, the French maintained small sailing ships to ensure communications and transport of goods and troops between Fort Frontenac, Niagara, and (later) Rouillé. From 1756, each ship had a detachment of soldiers assuming the duties of marines. This detail from a 1757 map shows the ships attractively painted and flying the all-white standards and pennants used by French warships before 1790. (Library and Archives Canada, NMC6433)

the mid-18th century. In 1750, Governor General La Jonquière instructed Captain Louis Legardeur de Repentigny to build a fort there for a small garrison. Its stockade walls covered an area of about $110ft^2$ ($11m^2$), enclosing several buildings and a redoubt. It was occupied by British troops in 1761.

The Sainte-Claire River connecting lakes Erie and Huron was also strategically important. In about 1686, Duluth built a stockade trading post called Fort Saint Joseph (Port Huron, Michigan), also called Fort Duluth, at the northwest end of the Sainte-Claire River facing Lake Huron. A small garrison of troops was posted there in September 1687. The fort being considered "useless" by the following year, it was evacuated and burned down on August 27, 1688, according to La Hontan. The importance of securing the Sainte-Claire River was recognized by French authorities and, in 1701, La Mothe Cadillac with a party of settlers arrived in the area. The initial settlers were former soldiers of Canada's colonial garrison that settled in the country after being released from service. A fort was built at "Le Détroit" on the western shore of the river and named Fort Pontchartrain, in honor of the current minister of the Navy, but it was usually called Fort Détroit (now the city of Detroit, Michigan). It initially consisted of a stockade square enclosure with bastions, which proved effective against an attack by the hostile Fox Indians in 1706. It was enlarged to form a rectangle by 1708, when its population was reckoned at being 63 souls. In 1712, the Fox Indians briefly besieged Détroit unsuccessfully. Thereafter, the town quickly grew and new streets were laid out in the following decades. Its rectangular stockade was farther extended to the west in 1740–41 and to the north in 1748–49, which expanded what was now becoming a town. By mid-century, Détroit and its area had about 800 inhabitants, some of which lived on farms built on both sides of the Sainte-Claire River. In October 1754, Commandant Jacques-Pierre Daneau de Muy considered Détroit indefensible and ordered Engineer Lt. Gaspard-Joseph Chaussegros de Léry to design a new enclosure with bastions to cover the curtain walls. By the spring of 1755, the fortifications of Détroit became quite different than they had been previously. No plan of this layout exists, but the new bastions were most likely added at each corner and in the middle of both the north and south curtain walls.

In 1758–59, Commandant François-Marie Picoté de Belestre had another expansion of the stockade constructed to the west, as well as a wide bastion outside both the north and south walls. The wide bastion on the north wall also had a small cavalier upon which were placed three small 3-pdr cannons and three small mortars, apparently the first substantial artillery mounted on Détroit's walls. Large bastions were now only at the corners on the south side facing the river. Détroit always had a fairly substantial military garrison, some of which was detached to other forts. On November 29, 1760, British troops arrived at Détroit to relieve its French garrison.

The southeastern end of Lake Erie had Fort Presqu'île which led to the French forts in the Ohio Valley to the south (see Fortress 75: *The Forts of New France in Northeast America 1600–1763*, René Chartrand, Osprey, Oxford, 2008). The western part of Lake Erie remained without forts until the mid-18th century, when authorities decided to secure the part of the lake that led to the Sainte-Claire River and to Détroit. Fort Sandusky was built in 1751 on the north side of Sandusky Bay, near the mouth of the Sandusky River (Ohio) that flows into Lake Erie. It consisted of a rectangular stockade with small corner bastions. Three years later, this fort was abandoned and its garrison moved to Fort Junandot, which had been built in 1752 on the east side of the mouth of the Sandusky River. Junandot was evacuated in 1759.

To the southwest of Lake Erie were a number of forts that depended on Détroit for troops and supplies. Fort Saint-Philippe des Miamis (Fort Wayne, Indiana), was built by order of Governor General Philippe de Vaudreuil in 1715 where the St Mary's and St Joseph rivers unite to form the Maumee River near a large Indian town. Previously, Fort Saint Joseph (Niles, Michigan) was often called Fort Miamis. From about 1715–20, Fort Miamis referred to Fort Saint-Philippe des Miamis. It protected trade routes as well as being an important trade post. It was also exposed to raids by hostile Indians. In 1747, while most of its garrison was at Détroit, the fort was taken, sacked and burned by a party

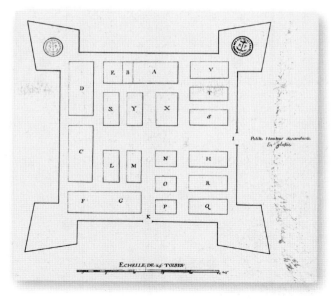

Plan of Détroit sent by Antoine de La Mothe Cadillac to the French authorities. It is very likely the actual layout of the town between 1701 and 1711. It later assumed a rectangular plan as it expanded. (Library and Archives Canada)

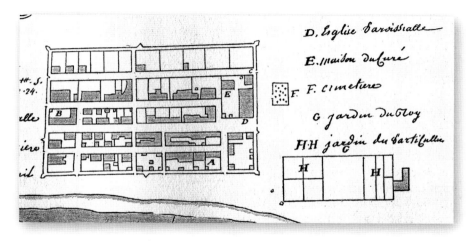

Plan of Détroit, August 20, 1749. This sketch drawn by Engineer Lt. Chaussegros de Léry shows the general layout of the town, which is enclosed by palisades. A: commandant's house, B: guard house and barracks, C: powder magazine, D: parish church, E: priest's house, F: cemetery, G: King's gardens. The streets are straight and laid out on a grid, permitting an orderly expansion. (Print after de Léry's sketch. Private collection)

Following the 1697 withdrawal of the French western garrisons, Antoine de La Mothe Cadillac went to France to persuade the government to reverse its decision and create instead a substantial new settlement at 'Le Détroit' to occupy the strategic location between lakes Erie and Huron. This would deny the British access to the rich fur trade of the upper lakes and become the hub of New France's western outposts. King Louis XIV approved the plan and Cadillac founded the city of Détroit on July 24, 1701. In this large painting by Leon Makielski originally commissioned for the Chicago World's Fair, Cadillac is shown presenting his proposal to the king. Amongst the interested onlookers behind the king are the Cardinal de Noailles, Count Pontchartrain, minister of the navy and colonies, and Madame de Maintenon. (Detroit Historical Museum)

Fort Sandusky, 1753. Built in the winter of 1750–51, this fort was sited on the northern bank of Lake Sandusky near the southern shore of Lake Erie (now Sandusky, Ohio) and abandoned about three years later. John Defever described it as made of "Pickett, having one officer and ten men, not above fifteen rods square, no cannon" in March 1752. In 1754, Engineer Lt. Chaussegros de Léry went there and made this sketch of its plan. It consisted of a square stockade measuring 60ft 3in. (19.5m) by 66ft 8in. (21.6m) with narrow corner bastions. Within was a large rectangular building with two chimneys. Its gate was less than 30ft (9m) from the lake's shore. The dotted line at right indicates a portage trail. (Print after de Léry's sketch. Private collection)

of English-allied Huron warriors. The fort was rebuilt during the summer of 1749. Three years later, two soldiers were killed defending the fort during a raid, but the hostile Indians were repulsed. In November 1760, a British garrison relieved the French troops. By then, the French garrison consisted of an officer, a sergeant and only seven soldiers. According to Lieutenant John Butler's description, the place consisted of "a good stockaded fort of 120 feet [36.5m] square with flankers [bastions or corner turrets] having ten houses" within, including the guardhouse (WO 34/90).

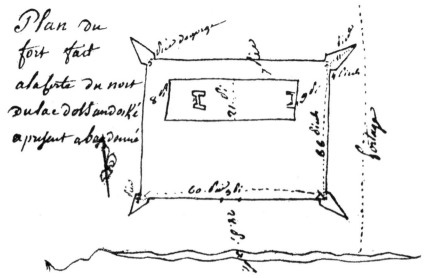

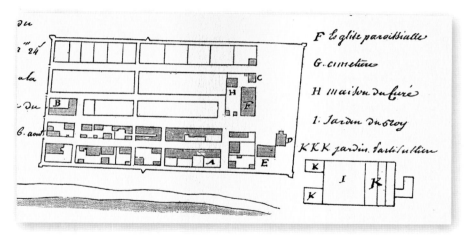

Fort Ouiatenon (near Lafayette, Indiana) was built in 1717 to counter British expansion in the Wabash River valley. It served as a trade and communication post. Archeological surveys done in the 1970s revealed that the fort was built on a rectangular plan with no corner bastions or turrets. The surveys also found that there had been two stockades, one measuring about 120 by 150ft (36.5 by 45.7m) and another outside measuring about 240 by 180ft (73.1 by 54.8m). It has been suggested that the smaller fort was the original and that it had been expanded. However, in 1761, when he arrived with a detachment of rangers to take it over, Lt. John Butler described the Fort Ouiatenon as "well stockaded of 100 feet wide and 150 long on the side of the Wabash River… this fort has fourteen houses in it… this fort is likewise on low land and last spring the water in the fort was four foot deep. Directly opposite the fort is an Indian village…" (WO 34/90). The exterior wall may therefore have been an outer picket line. The British abandoned it in 1763.

Lake Michigan

From the 1630s, French explorers traveled in the area of the Straits of Mackinac. In the late 1660s, French missionaries noted its outstanding strategic location, being situated at the narrows uniting lakes Huron and Michigan as well as being relatively close to the entrance to Lake Superior. It was already an ideal trading area for Indian nations, and missionaries were staying there as early as 1671. In that year, Jacques Marquette built a mission named Saint-Ignace on the north shore of the straits (St Ignace, Michigan). He was soon joined by explorers and traders, resulting in a small French village being built. From 1683, a small stockade was built around the mission and the French traders' houses, and was

Fort Michilimackinac, c.1685. This model is a conjectural reconstruction of what the early mission and trader's fort of Saint-Ignace might have looked like. This first Fort Michilimackinac was located on the north shore of the Mackinac Straits. Defenses were minimal, consisting of little more than a picket fence. Other posts such as the one at Baie Verte (Green Bay, Wisconsin) probably had the same general appearance. (Fort Michilimackinac Museum)

seen by La Hontan four years later. In 1690, Fort de Buade was built, possibly on a hill overlooking Moran Bay. It served as the main French base for attacks on the Seneca Iroquois allied to the English. A small garrison was posted there in 1688 and withdrawn in 1698. Traders continued to roam the area, and eventually the French authorities determined that an official presence was required at the straits of Mackinac. In 1715, a commandant with a detachment of troops was sent to build a new stockade fort situated on the south shore of the straits of Mackinac facing Lake Michigan (near Mackinaw City, Michigan). Fort Michilimackinac was built on a rectangular plan, with small corner bastions. Its palisade expanded as time passed and more houses were built within. Its European population in the mid-18th century came to about 150 souls including its small garrison of about 20 to 30 soldiers. Some 400 Indians lived in several villages established nearby. During the early 1750s, the northern palisade facing Lake Michigan appears to have been expanded, and possibly the palisade on the southern side also, changing the layout of the fort's walls to a somewhat polygonal plan. In 1761, a British garrison relieved the French troops.

One of the early French sites of the western Great Lakes was at the present Green Bay, Wisconsin. The long bay on the upper western side of Lake Michigan had already been named "La Baye des Puants" (literally: Stinker's Bay, also interpreted as "Bay of the Stinking Water") by early *coureurs des bois* when, in 1634, Jean Nicolet landed on the shores of the bay wearing a silk Mandarin robe, as he hoped he had reached the shores of China! He was met by rather startled Winnebago Indians, but everyone soon proceeded to trade at a small post Nicolet established there. The place became known as "La Baye Verte" (Green Bay) and more simply as "La Baye" (the Bay). The first permanent French presence came in 1669 with the arrival of Jesuit father Claude Allouez who built the St François Xavier mission there. Following the 1670s explorations of Father Marquette and Louis Jolliet of the upper Mississippi River, La Baye assumed a strategic position on the water route to the south and became an important trading center and rendezvous site.

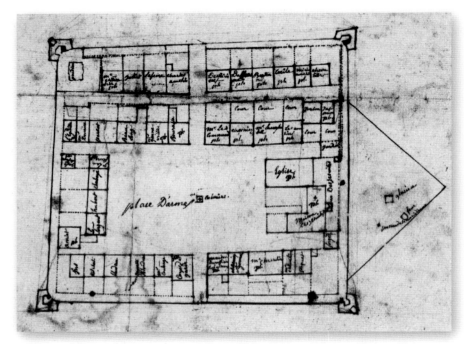

Plan of Fort Michilimackinac, 1749. Drawn by visiting Ensign Michel Chartier de Lobtinière, this remarkable plan shows the second fort established since 1715 on the south shore of the Straits of Mackinac laid out in a square plan enclosed by stockade walls with small bastions at the corners. A small powder magazine is at the upper left corner. The "place d'armes" (main square) had a well at its center, a church with the lodgings of the Jesuit missionaries at right, the guardhouse near the gate below, and the streets are straight and well defined. Most other houses belonged to traders, but one at left was for a sergeant and another for the commandant. The triangular lot outside (at right) had an icehouse and a baking oven. (Library and Archives Canada, NMC12806)

In 1684, Nicolas Perrot was named commandant of the area and he had a small, fortified trading post built at La Baye. This fort deteriorated and was later abandoned because of warfare with the Fox Indians, but, in 1717, Fort La Baye was rebuilt and a military garrison was posted there. It proved to be an important base of operations and supplies during the wars against the Fox nations by the French and their many Indian allies. In 1732, the fort was abandoned and destroyed, but it was reconstructed the following year. A small garrison was posted there under the command of one or two officers. During the winter of 1759 an uprising of Menominee Indians occurred at Green Bay, which killed 22 French soldiers before it was put down. The Menominee soon regretted their actions and seven of the participants were sent to Montréal for punishment. With Canada being overwhelmed by British and American colonial armies, the garrison of Green Bay evacuated to Illinois. On October 12, 1761, a detachment of British troops arrived to find "the fort quite rotten, the stockade ready to fall, the houses without cover" according to Lieutenant James Gorrell, who renamed it Fort Edward Augustus.

The southern part of Lake Michigan was not as strategic as its northern part. Nevertheless, La Salle built the small stockade of Fort Miamis in November 1679, where the St Joseph River flows into Lake Michigan (St Joseph, Michigan). It was named after the Indian nation in that area. This temporary fort should not be confused with the later Fort Saint Joseph (near Niles, Michigan, 20 miles or 32km upriver), initially called Fort Miamis, and the Fort Miamis (Fort Wayne, Indiana) on the Maumee River. A Fort Chicago, or "Chicagou", was built in 1683 by La Salle's men on the site of the present city of Chicago. It appears to have been a small trader's fort with a fairly sizeable Jesuit mission, but few if any troops appear to have been permanently posted there. It was later said to have been enlarged with a stockade, two houses of squared timber and two houses of posts in the ground. According to De Tonti, "the fort of Chicagou" was where Captain de La Durantaye "commanded" in late 1685. It was razed some years later, probably by the

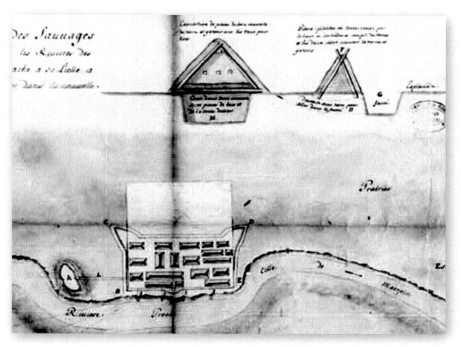

Plan of a fortified Fox Indian town besieged by the French and allied Indians in the fall of 1730. It featured curtain walls made of earth reinforced with logs, bastions, and a moat. All these features borrowed from European military architecture. The buildings inside were "A-frame" log huts covered with earth and grass that made them fireproof. Under the buildings was an elaborate system of tunnels that linked them all together. The town was taken at great loss of life to the Fox when they fled. Nevertheless, the Indians' fortifications impressed King's Engineer Chaussegros de Léry, who made an illustrated report of it. (Archives Nationales [Aix-en-Provence, France], Colonies, C11A, 126)

Fort Michilimackinac, 1749

1690s (Baudouin, 24). The Jesuit mission remained and was described in 1699 by Father Pinet as "the house of the reverend fathers … built on the shore of the river having on one side the lake and on the other a lovely prairie." Nearby were two large Indian villages.

Fort Saint Joseph (Niles, Michigan) was initially a Jesuit mission established on the northeast bank of the St Joseph River in October 1686. Before the 1720s, it was also called Fort Miamis, which has caused some confusion with Fort Saint-Philippe (at Fort Wayne, Indiana) usually called Fort Miamis from the 1720s. In 1691, Governor General Frontenac dispatched Augustin Le Gardeur de Courtemanche there with a dozen soldiers, with instructions to build a fort and be its commandant. The fort was near the Jesuit's mission and consisted of houses for the commandant and the soldiers with storehouses for the fur trade enclosed by a stockade with two gates, one to the north and one to the south. In 1698, the military garrison was evacuated, but the fur traders remained and the troops eventually came back. The fort served as the French diplomatic, military, commercial, and religious center in its area until October 1761 when a detachment of British troops replaced the French garrison.

Lake Superior

The earliest post on the shores of Lake Superior was the mission of Saint-Esprit, established by missionaries in 1660 at La Pointe, at the southwestern end of the lake (near Ashland, Wisconsin). The following year, the stockade Fort Chequemagon (various spellings) was built there by explorers and traders Radisson and Des Groseilliers. This fort appears to have been accidentally destroyed by fire in about 1670. In 1692, Governor General Frontenac had a new Fort Chequemagon built and garrisoned, but it was

Map of the rivers in the northern Great Plains, according to La Hontan's travels, 1688. This fascinating document is partly based on maps drawn on hides by the "Gnacsitares" Indians that shows a very long river, the "Rivière Longue" that becomes the "Rivière Morte" (Dead River) as it reaches the mountains with a portage (marked by little crosses) to another river farther west. The identity of this river appears to be the Minnesota, and the Indians met may have been the Dakotas. At the lower left is a sketch of a boat used by the distant "Tanuglauk" Indian nation that had up to 200 rowers, and a view of their houses, both of which are amazingly reminiscent of the Indian nations of the Pacific northwestern coasts. Starting in "Misilimakinak" in September 1688, La Hontan traveled with ten soldiers and Ottawa Indian guides as far as the dotted double line on the "Rivière Longue" and also crossed lakes Superior and Michigan (called "Ilinois" on this map). At the lower right can be seen little squares indicating Fort Crèvecoeur and Fort Miamis. (Private collection)

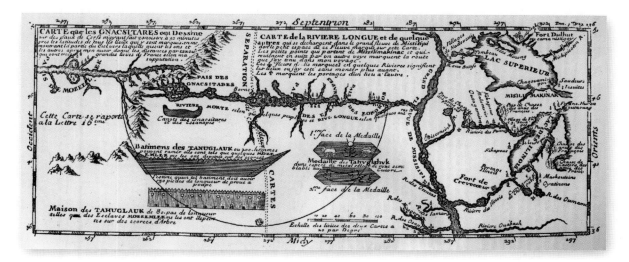

C   FORT MICHILIMACKINAC, 1749

Michilimackinac was the most important French trading and military post in the upper Great Lakes. French communities in the New World were, like the Spanish, planned on a grid with straight streets with a central "Place d'armes" or plaza. The church and the official's lodgings and offices would face this open area. Fort Michilimackinac's fortifications were always simple and initially consisted of wooden stockade walls built on a rectangular plan with small corner bastions to provide protection against hostile Indian raids or disturbances from groups of drunken individuals. Probate records also mention a "chemin de ronde" outside the stockade for sentries. Like in some other frontier towns, notably Détroit, the walls expanded as more houses were built on newly laid-out streets. It had six guns, probably of small caliber and mounted in the small bastions.

abandoned in about 1698. In 1718, Governor General Vaudreuil ordered the fort rebuilt and garrisoned by a detachment of troops. It was often also called Fort La Pointe. Its main purpose was to secure the fur trade and communications in that area. It was located on the south end of Madeleine Island. This fort appears to have been abandoned and destroyed following the surrender of Canada. Since about 1680, Fort Sainte-Croix was built by traders on the St Croix River (Wisconsin) near the portage from the Mississippi River to Lake Superior. This outpost appears to have operated during the whole French regime.

The Fort Kaministiquia (various spellings) trade post was established in about 1679 by Daniel Greysolon Duluth at the mouth of the Kaministiquia River on the northwest shore of Lake Superior (at Thunder Bay, Ontario). Another fortified trading post, which Duluth named Fort La Tourette after his brother, Claude Greysolon, Sieur de La Tourette, was established around 1684 at the northeast end of Lake Nipigon according to Jaillot's 1685 map, and Fort des Français the next year at the forks of the Albany and Kenogami rivers. These outposts did not have military garrisons and were abandoned during the 1690s. In 1717, Fort Kaministiquia was rebuilt to counter possible penetration and influence by the English in Hudson Bay. It was mainly a trade post headed by a military commandant with a few soldiers. The fort at Lake Nipigon was also reestablished under the name of Fort Nipigon. In 1728, Lieutenant Pierre Gaultier de La Vérendrye was Kaministiquia's area commandant and the information he obtained from western Indians led him to use this fort as a base of operations for explorations in the Prairies. The forts on Lake Superior were abandoned following the surrender of Canada in September 1760.

To the southwest of Lake Superior were a number of small stockade forts built on the upper Mississippi River to trade with the Sioux Indians. Fort Saint-Nicolas (Prairie-du-Chien, Wisconsin) was a fur trade post built by Nicolas Perrot in about 1685 at or near the mouth of the Wisconsin River, still operating in 1755 but reported abandoned and destroyed by 1762. Fort Trempealeau (literally meaning "soaked in water") and Fort Saint Antoine were also built by Perrot on the area of Lake Pepin (a widening of the Mississippi River at the border of the states of Wisconsin and Minnesota) in

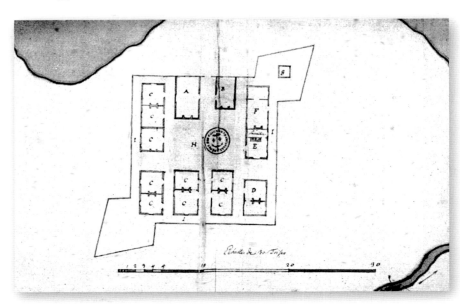

Plan of Fort Beauharnois, 1727. The fort was about 17 *toises* square (31.11m²) with two bastions, one of which had a small powder magazine. Within were eight buildings that included a chapel, a guardhouse, an officer's residence, a soldiers' barracks, a storehouse, and traders' quarters. This fort was abandoned in the 1740s, but another named Fort La Jonquière was built in the same area in 1750. (Library and Archives Canada)

about 1685 and, on May 8, 1689, Perrot even staged a ceremony at Fort Saint Antoine to take formal possession of the upper Mississippi for France. In 1700, trader and explorer Pierre Le Sueur explored some of the Minnesota River and, in the fall, built Fort L'Huillier on the shore of the "Rivière Bleue" (now the Blue Earth River, Minnesota) south of its confluence with the Minnesota River. It consisted of two or three cabins enclosed by a stockade. Le Sueur returned to France in 1702 and the fort was abandoned. In 1727, Fort Beauharnois (or Beauharnais, near Frontenac, Minnesota), named in honor of the governor general of New France, but often called "Les Sioux", was built by traders at Lake Pepin near the Mississippi's shore and was flooded that year. Because the Fox Indians had many Sioux friends, it was a dangerous place. The traders did not dare venture outside the fort, so they lost money and left the place in 1729. Governor General Beauharnois wanted to keep it in operation by sending a commandant and a second officer "with a few soldiers" to keep an eye on the Fox and Sioux Indians. According to La Vérendrye, it could draw trade from Assiniboine Indians farther west (C11A, 51, 54). Following the defeat of the Fox Indians, the fort was rebuilt on higher ground in about 1731 as a garrisoned post with a commandant. It consisted of a square stockade with two large bastions at opposite ends. Trade was very good, but there were some violent incidents and two traders were killed by the Sioux. Commandant Le Gardeur de Saint-Pierre was told by the fur traders that they "preferred losing their business than their lives," and the fort was evacuated in March 1736 (C11A, 67). In 1750, a new fort called Fort La Jonquière (not to be confused with the fort of the same name built on the Prairies, see below), also named in honor of the current governor general of New France, was built in roughly the same area, perhaps the same site as the former Fort Beauharnois. Its stockade may have had four blockhouse-style bastions. It was abandoned following the fall of Canada. East of this fort was Fort Marin, an apparently temporary outpost built by Captain Paul Marin de La Malgue in 1750.

THE PRAIRIES AND THE "WESTERN SEA"

At the beginning of the 18th century, what lay west of Lake Superior remained a mystery. As early as 1671, Sieur de Saint-Lusson, a military officer, had taken official possession at Sault Sainte-Marie of "the West" for the King of France. Except for Henry Kelsey's 1691 exploratory foray into the prairies from Hudson Bay, the West remained largely a blank space on maps. In Versailles, princes were also intrigued and especially wondered where the vast prairies would reach the "Mer de l'Ouest" (Western Sea) – the Pacific Ocean. Cartographer Guillaume Delisle even claimed it was an inland sea with an isthmus on the Pacific. In 1730, a proposal arrived at Versailles to explore the prairies and reach the sea. Lieutenant Pierre Gaultier de La Vérendrye, commandant of the outpost Fort Kaministiquia, proposed to finance the expedition by gradually establishing fur trade forts as he moved west. A new trade sector would be created ensuring a French presence on the prairies, thus excluding the English traders who might come down from Hudson Bay and secure alliances with Plains Indians. Versailles approved and, in 1731, La Vérendrye with four officer-cadets (three of whom were his sons), a missionary, a few soldiers, and some traders headed for the Great Plains. During the next decades, they built a number of forts as they moved westward. The search for the western sea reached a climax when, in early

Lt. Pierre Gaultier de La Vérendrye pondering information on the vast western prairies as related by Ochagach, a Cree Indian that he befriended at Fort Kaministiquia situated on the north-western shore of Lake Superior, c.1728–29. Their meeting turned out to be a most important event in North American history as it led to the explorations into the Canadian and American West up to the Rocky Mountains as well as contacts and trade with the Plains Indian nations. There is no detailed description of the fort, but this illustration is an interesting evocation of what the interior of such outposts might have looked like. La Vérendrye's and Ochagach's personal appearance are unknown and unlikely to have been as illustrated in this plate. La Vérendrye, for instance, would probably have been clean-shaven and wearing a cloth capot rather than a fringed deerskin jacket. (Print after E. J. Dinsmore. Private collection)

January 1743, officer-cadets Louis-Joseph and François de La Vérendrye came within sight of the Rocky Mountains (probably south of Sheridan, Wyoming). They could not cross them and the western sea remained elusive. La Vérendrye was eventually succeeded by other officers and the "Poste de l'Ouest" (western post), as the network of forts became known, operated until 1759–60. The forts built on the prairies were simple stockade structures, "respectable only to Indians" according to Bougainville.

Fort Saint-Pierre was built in 1731 on the western bank of Rainy Lake (probably at Pither's Point in Fort Frances, Ontario). It consisted of a "fort with two gates on opposite sides. The interior length of the side is fifty feet with two bastions. There are two main buildings each having two rooms with double chimneys. Around these buildings is a sentry's road seven feet wide. In one of the bastions a storehouse and a powder magazine have been made. And there is a double row of stakes, thirteen feet out of the ground" (Beauharnois to minister, 15 October 1732, Bibliothèque Nationale, NAF 2552).

Fort Saint-Charles was built in the fall of 1732 (about 2 miles or 3km from American Point, Minnesota). It was described in 1732 as measuring "one hundred feet [square] with four bastions. There is a house for the missionary, a church, and another house for the commandant, four main buildings with chimneys, a powder magazine and a storehouse. The are also two gates on opposite sides, and a watch tower, and the stakes are in double row and are fifteen feet out of the ground" (C11E, 16).

About 6 miles (10km) south of Selkirk, Manitoba was Fort de la Fourche aux Roseaux, a small post built in 1733 where one of La Vérendrye's sons, killed by Indians, was buried. The first Fort Maurepas was built during the

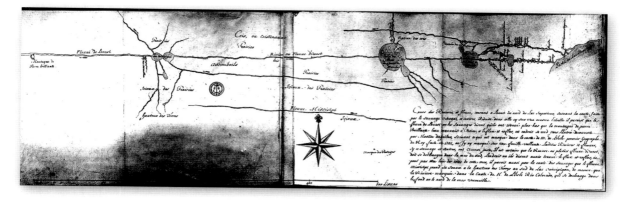

summer and fall of 1734 on the west bank of the Red River, about five leagues from Lake Winnipeg (probably about 6 miles or 10km north of Selkirk, Manitoba). It was a large fort, with a palisade made of oak. In 1740, it was transferred from its site on the Red River and rebuilt at the mouth of Lake Winnipeg (probably near Pine Falls). This fort appears to have been active until the late 1750s.

Fort la Reine was built from October 3 to October 15, 1738, on the north shore of the Assiniboine river (now Portage la Prairie, Manitoba). It was strategically located on Indian trade routes. Amongst the buildings within its stockade were a guardhouse, a residence for the commandant, and a powder magazine. The fort was evacuated in February 1752, burned by the Indians in July, restored thereafter by the French, and definitively abandoned in 1758.

Fort Rouge or Fort La Fourche was built in October 1738 on the south-west banks where the Assiniboine and the Red rivers meet. By 1749, it had been abandoned because of its proximity to Fort de La Reine.

The first Fort Paskoya was built in about 1739, close to the "First Forks" where the Saskatchewan River flows into Cedar Lake. It was abandoned in

Map of the western prairies, c.1729–30. This map was drawn by Lt. Pierre Gaultier de La Vérendrye according to information related by Ochagach at Fort Kaministiquia. This data was originally on bark maps that are now lost. The orientation and scale on Indian maps is different than on European maps. For instance, distance is calculated by time rather than space; the fewer difficulties encountered meant faster travel and hence less space on the map. (Library and Archives Canada, NMC6415)

The La Vérendrye brothers reach the Rocky Mountains in early January 1743. This event is reputed to have occurred in the area of present-day Sheridan in Wyoming. Both brothers were cadets in the Compagnies Franches de la Marine detached to the western prairie outposts. (Library and Archives Canada, C70247)

Detail from an extraordinary map of the western part of Canada published in Paris by Philippe Buache in 1754. It tried to compile reports sent to France by La Vérendrye and other officers that described their explorations, and also included the intelligence given by Indians on their maps, including Ochagach's. Lac Bourbon is now Lake Winnipeg and the Poskoyac River (top left) is the North Saskatchewan River that divides in two and reaches the Rocky Mountains. So does the Missouri River (bottom) that "flows into the Mississippi" farther south. On the left is the "Mer de l'ouest" (the Western Sea) – the Pacific Ocean – that Indians rightly claimed existed past the mountains. Naturally, the distances on this map are wildly inaccurate and should be much greater as one moves west. (Library and Archives Canada, NMC13295)

1743, but the second Fort Bourbon was built on its site in 1750, probably from the ruins of the old Fort Puskoya. This second Fort Bourbon was eventually pillaged and burned by the Indians in 1758.

The first Fort Dauphin was built in 1741 by Pierre de La Vérendrye at the mouth of the Mossy River and Lake Winnipegossis (near Winnipegossis, Manitoba). Some years later, a second Fort Dauphin located northwest of Dauphin Lake on the Mossy River replaced the initial fort. It was still operated by traders in 1759.

The second Fort Paskoya was built around 1750–53 on the shores of the Saskatchewan River (The Pas, Manitoba). On May 19, 1755, English explorer Anthony Hendry traveling east on the river came upon Fort Puskoya and described what he saw: "The Master [possibly Captain Louis-François de Lacorne] invited me in to sup with him, and was very Kind. He is dressed very genteel, but the men wear nothing but thin drawers, & stripped cotton shirts ruffled at the hands & breast. This House has been long a place of Trade belonging to the French, & named Basquea. It is 26 [English] feet long; 12 feet wide; 9 feet high to the ridge; having a sloping roof; the Walls Log on Log; the top covered with Birch-rind, fastened together with Willows, & divided into three apartments: one for Trading goods, one for Furs, and the third they dwell in." It was probably surrounded by a rudimentary stockade or fence. This fort was abandoned in the spring of 1759.

There were also secondary posts: La Barrière (1733) on the Winnipeg River (Manitoba), Vermillion (1736) at the mouth of the Vermillion River (Minnesota), La Fourche des Assiniboines (Winnipeg, Manitoba), Portage de l'Île (1750) at the fork of the English and Winnipeg rivers (Ontario), Tête de Boeuf (1752) on the west side of Lake Winnipeg, and La Biche (1753) on La Biche River (Saskatchewan). The most westerly posts were on the shores of the Saskatchewan River. After Fort Paskoya (described above) came forts La Jonquière (1751), Nipawi, and, the most westerly, La Corne (about 1753), which was probably near the fork where the river split into two: the North Saskatchewan and the South Saskatchewan rivers. This is the center of the present province of Saskatchewan.

As the military men and traders advanced westward, it was realized that there was no inland sea and that a mighty mountain range blocked the way. Following La Vérendrye's extraordinary exploration, few ventured farther, but, in Canada, the quest for the Western Sea was never quite given up. On July 20, 1793, Alexander Mackenzie from Montréal finally achieved the first transcontinental crossing north of Mexico and reached the Pacific Ocean at the present Bella Coola, British Columbia. On a rock facing the Pacific, he could at last inscribe: "from Canada, by land."

Louisiana

In 1682, Robert Cavelier de La Salle reached the Gulf of Mexico, took possession for France of the newly explored country and christened it "Louisiane" after the name of King Louis XIV. A first attempt to settle at the mouth of the Mississippi on the Gulf Coast ended in tragedy with La Salle's murder during the late 1680s. In 1699, the Canadian-born naval officer Pierre Le Moyne d'Iberville built a fort at Biloxi Bay that became the base for other French settlements in lower Louisiana in various, and sometimes unfortunate, colonization schemes. Meanwhile, some Canadians were attracted by the lush and warm "pays des Illinois" on the upper Mississippi Valley and started to settle there from the end of the 17th century. Canadian officials initially administered this new area until September 27, 1717, when the king decreed that henceforth, the "Illinois Country" would be part of Louisiana. This coincided with the royal wish to grant all of Louisiana to a private monopoly company. Of these, after several financial crashes, the "Compagnie des Indes" (which also had monopolies in India and Africa) proved to be the most stable, but found Louisiana unprofitable and awkward to administer. Following the Natchez uprising, the company handed back its Louisiana monopoly to the royal government on January 23, 1731, keeping only the exclusive rights on the exportation of beaver pelts for all of New France. From then on, Louisiana was under direct royal administration, just like the other French domains in America until the Treaty of Paris of 1763. Unlike Canada, Louisiana was not invaded by Anglo-American armies during the Seven Years War, although some of its troops detached from the Illinois forts were involved in the Ohio and Niagara campaigns.

The Illinois country and upper Mississippi

In the middle of January 1680, explorer Robert Cavelier de La Salle and his men were in the area of present-day Peoria, Illinois, and decided to build a fort there to protect the Ilini Indian nation from their Iroquois enemies. They named it Fort Crèvecoeur. La Salle left a remarkably detailed description of the fort. Its site:

> was a little hillock about 540 feet from the bank of the [Illinois] river; up to the foot of the hillock the river expanded every time that there fell a heavy rain. Two wide and deep ravines enclosed two other sides of the hillock and half of the fourth, which I caused to be closed completely by a ditch that joined the two ravines. Along the outer edge of the ravines, I caused to be placed good chevaux-de-frise [a series of heavy timbers placed in a line, interlaced with other diagonal timbers that often had pointed tips], had the slopes of the

hillock to be cut down all around, and with the earth thus excavated I caused to be built on the top of a parapet capable of covering a man, the whole covered [or rather, lined] from the foot of the hillock to the top of the parapet with long beams, the lower ends of which were in groove between two long pieces of wood which extended all around the foot of the elevation; and I caused the top of these beams to be fastened by other long cross-beams held in place by tenons and mortises with other pieces of wood that projected through the parapet. In front of that work I caused to be planted, everywhere, pointed posts 25 feet in height, one foot in diameter, driven 3 feet in the ground, pegged to the cross-beams that fastened the top of the beams and provided with a fraise [a fraise was an obstacle consisting of palissades projecting horizontally] at the top 2½ feet long to prevent [being attacked by] surprise.

The rest of his description refers to the building of two lodgings for his men in the two corners most important for the defense, a forge in the third corner for the forge, and a lodging for the Recollet missionaries in the fourth corner. La Salle had his tent and that of Henri De Tonti placed in the center of the fort. The Iroquois were nevertheless an overwhelming menace and the fort was abandoned in April.

Fort Saint-Louis (Starved Rock State Park, Illinois) was built in late 1682 and early 1683 by La Salle and Henri De Tonti at the lower rapids of the Illinois River. It was located on top of a 125ft-high (41m) cliff called "Starved Rock" that was steep on three sides like a castle's wall. The French cleared trees at the top and built lodgings and storehouses that were protected by a palisade. The fort controlled this strategic river, which was then the main link between Canada and Louisiana. Many friendly Indians initially gathered there, but they eventually left because of pressure from Iroquois war parties, and the fort was abandoned in 1691. French traders later reoccupied it since some were reported being there in 1718, but, three years later, it was clear that the fort had again been abandoned when Father Charlevoix saw the remains of its wrecked palisade.

Fort Pimitoui, also called Fort Saint-Louis, (probably near the narrows at the head of lower Peoria Lake, Illinois) was built during the winter of 1691–92 by Henri De Tonti and Francois Dauphin de La Forest. The French and Indians moved here from the first Fort Saint-Louis (at Starved Rock). Around April 1693, Father Jacques Gravier re-established the Mission of the Immaculate Conception at Fort Pimitoui, said to have been "the finest mission of the Jesuit fathers" with over 800 Indians living there six years later. De Tonti and La Forest were deprived of their concession in 1702, but the fort seems to have continued on as a trade post. In 1718, an officer, a sergeant, and ten soldiers from Canada were posted there, but were ordered withdrawn in May 1719 following the transfer of Illinois to Louisiana (C11A, 41). A commandant with a small detachment of Louisiana troops was later posted at Pimitoui until the end of the Seven Years War.

French explorers visited Cahokia from 1673 and a mission was established there in 1699. It was the first permanent European settlement in the Illinois country. A small fort was later built there and was described in 1723 as a miserable stockade with a small detachment consisting of an officer with six soldiers as its garrison. Captain Bossu mentions Fort Cahokia as still being garrisoned in the 1750s. It was not important militarily, but, by 1760, some 300 settlers lived there. Its small garrison had been withdrawn and the stockade burned down by the time British troops arrived in August 1766.

A trade post was first established in October 1702 in the area of the present city of Vincennes, Indiana, and thrived for a couple of years. However, following the death of its founder, Juchereau, and the perceived hostility of some Indians, the post was abandoned. Fort Vincennes (also called "Fort Ouabache") was constructed in 1731–32 as a garrisoned trade post to secure the lower Wabash River valley from possible Anglo-American incursions. It initially consisted of a stockade with only two houses within. It bore the name of its first commandant: François-Marie Bissot, sieur de Vincennes. From 1736, his successor, commandant de Saint-Ange, made the fort a major trade center, notably by moving it to higher ground in 1738 (C13A, 23). In 1752, following small Indian raids on nearby French settlers and their slaves, the fort's stockade was enlarged to enclose the church, the presbytery, and houses of some of the French inhabitants (VP, 113). Following the end of the Seven Years War, the fort passed to the British who renamed it Fort Sackville in 1766.

Founded in 1703, Kaskasia was one of the earliest French settlements in the Mississippi Valley's Illinois country and became a major settlement and river port. There were initially no fortifications until 1733 when a wooden stockade was built on the hill overlooking the town. There were various proposals to build a more substantial fort in the following decades. In 1751,

Fort Kaskaskia, 1764. Pittman described the fort "which was burned down in October 1766" as being "on the summit of a high rock opposite the village, and on the other [eastern] side of the river; it was an obtangular quadrangle, of which the exterior polygon measured two hundred and ninety by two hundred and fifty-one feet; it was built of very thick squared timber, and dovetailed at the angles. An officer and twenty soldiers are quartered in the village" which also had "two companies of militia." (Detail of a plan after Pittman's *Present state…* 1770)

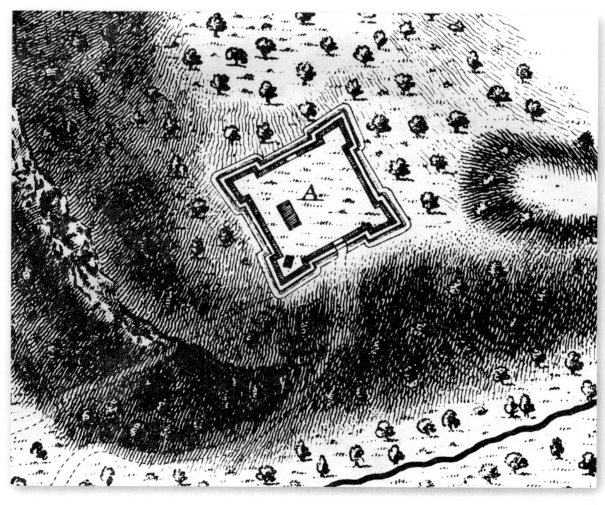

Governor Vaudreuil raised the possibility of moving the district HQ from Fort de Chartres to a new fort that would be built in Kaskaskia, but it was finally decided to rebuild Fort de Chartres with stone instead. However, although construction was started at that time, it seems to have been interrupted to concentrate on Fort de Chartres. Possibly in 1758 or 1759, Fort Kaskaskia was rebuilt by order of Commandant Macarty (C11A, 105). Philip Pittman sketched and described it a few years later. It was destroyed by fire in 1766, apparently by Kaskasia's inhabitants who did not wish to leave it to the British.

In 1713–14, Ensign Étienne Veniard de Bourgmond explored the Missouri River as far as the Platte River. In 1723, he came back to the area with about 40 men and built Fort Orléans on the north shore of the Missouri River (in the general area of Marshall, Missouri) as a garrisoned trade post. It was laid out on a square plan with bastions. The fort was in operation for about three years until taken by the Indians "and all the French murdered" according to Le Page du Pratz. In the spring and summer of 1744, another fort was built by Joseph Deruisseau to conduct trade with the Indians farther west on the Missouri River (in the area of Leavenworth, Kansas). It was named Fort Cavagnial in honor of Louisiana governor Pierre François de Rigaud, marquis de Vaudreuil-Cavagnial, although the governor initially named it La Trinité, but others called it Fort Cavagnial. The fort was constructed of logs, was 80ft^2 (8m^2), with bastions at each corner, the rear bastions being "storied" which probably meant a roofed second-level structure above the bastion. Inside were a commandant's house, a guardhouse, a powder magazine, a trader's house, and a house for lodging the employees of the traders, all made of mud-covered logs. The post's garrison consisted of a commandant, eight to ten soldiers, and several traders. The fort's trade thrived, both with the Indians and with the Spanish at Santa Fe (New Mexico) until the 1750s when increasingly hostile Indians and the effects of the Seven Years War

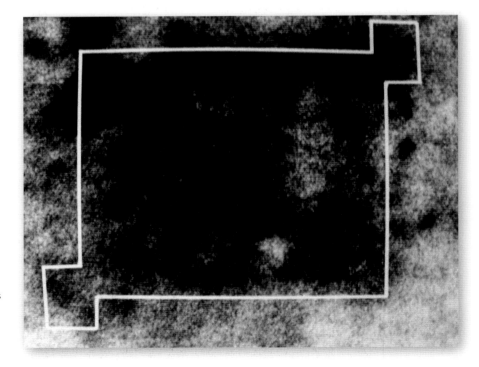

Areal view of the first Fort de Chartres, 1720–25 with its curtain walls and two bastions outlined in white. A US Army Corps of Engineers pilot took this photo in 1928. (Fort de Chartres Museum)

brought about a gradual decline. The only military action there appears to have occurred in about 1752 when soldiers killed two Missouri Indians who raided a nearby corral to steal horses. The fort's isolation may have been too much for some soldiers, but desertion was not much of an option. In 1753, three soldiers deserted but were killed by the Indians. The fort was abandoned in 1764 and was not occupied by the Spanish. It was reported as decaying, but its remnants were seen by Lewis and Clark in 1804 and by Colonel Long in 1819. The present locations of Fort Orléans and Fort Cavagnial remain uncertain.

There were three successive fortifications named Fort de Chartres (near Prairie du Rocher, Illinois). It was an important military and administrative post that acted as the capital of the Illinois country, being the residence of the area's commandant. The first fort, located within "a musket shot" of the Mississippi River, was built by Captain Boisbriant in 1720–21 and its garrison of 100 men. It consisted of a slightly rectangular palisade fort with two small bastions commanding the curtain walls at opposite ends. It measured 192 English feet (58m) on each side. There is no detailed record of the buildings within, but there was a commandant's residence, a storehouse, and a trade store. This fort quickly deteriorated and, in March 1725, a new fort was built near the first fort, and finished by February 1726. It was about 160ft^2 (15m^2) with four small bastions, its curtain walls apparently made of a double row of stakes with musket loopholes at intervals of 5ft (1.5m). A small chapel and a small hospital were outside. Its location remains unknown. This fort too deteriorated, probably in large part because of occasional flooding from the Mississippi River. By the 1740s, the fort was reported as being in bad shape and, in 1747, most of its garrison was moved to temporary quarters at nearby Kaskaskia.

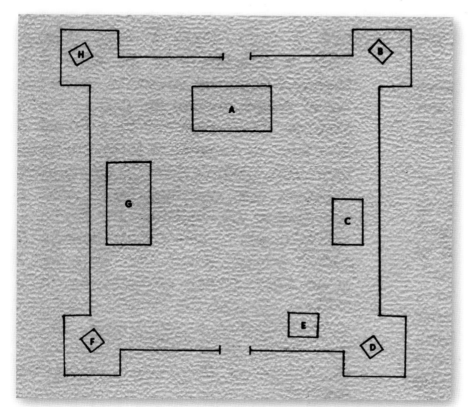

Plan of the second Fort de Chartres, 1725 to c.1754. A: commandant's residence, B: stable, C: building of unspecified use, D: pavilion and henhouse, E: guardhouse, F: prison, G: barracks and forge, H: powder magazine. (Illinois Department of Conservation, Division of Historic Sites)

D

D   FORT DE CHARTRES, c.1756–65

The first two forts named de Chartres were wooden stockade structures built on the shores of the Mississippi River, the timbers of which rotted when they were not washed away by the frequent floods of that mighty river. Furthermore, it was hardly an impressive headquarters for the French government's officials and troops in the Illinois country (or Upper Louisiana). This changed from 1752 when governor Vaudreuil decided that the third Fort de Chartres would be much larger and built of stone quarried nearby. Work started in 1753 under the direction of King's Engineer Jean-Baptiste Saucier and the fort was essentially completed three years later. While it was not designed to withstand a force equipped with heavy artillery, its stone walls and bastions made it possibly the most powerful fort between Fort Niagara in the Great Lakes region and Fort Mobile on the Gulf of Mexico.

Governor Vaudreuil of Louisiana decided in 1752 that a new and much larger Fort de Chartres would be built, this time of stone, capable of lodging 300 soldiers and holding a year's rations in its storehouses. Work started in 1753, but there was some hesitation in France over the cost of this new fort and, the following year, officials ordered the cancellation of its construction. Governor Kerlerc, who replaced Vaudreuil, protested that it was too late to cancel because the building materials had been bought and the greater part of the work had been finished. It was a spacious and impressive-looking fort built on a square plan with large bastions measuring, according to a 1975 archeological plan, about 500 English feet (152m) to a side from bastion tip to bastion tip. Pittman described it as follows in about 1764:

It is built of stone and plastered over, and is only designed as a defense against the Indians, the walls being two feet two inches thick, and pierced with loop-holes at regular distances, and with two post-holes for cannon in the faces, and two in the flanks of each bastion; the ditch has never been finished; the entrance to the fort is through a very handsome rustic gate: within the wall is a small banquette, raised three feet, for the men to stand on when they fire through the loop-holes. The buildings within the fort are, the commandant's and commissary's houses, the magazine of stores, corps de garde, and two barracks; these occupy the square. Within the gorges of the bastions are, a powder magazine, a bakehouse, a prison, in the lower floor of which are four dungeons, and in the upper rooms, and an

Fort de Chartre's southeast bastion features the powder magazine built during the 1750s (at center right). This very sturdy building did not collapse like others in the fort after it was abandoned, and was restored during the 20th century. The foundations of barracks and other buildings have been stabilized and "shadowed" by timber frames to indicate their general appearance. Note also the bastions and curtain walls with loopholes for muskets and embrasures for cannons.

out-house belonging to the commandant. The commandant's house is thirty-two yards long, and ten broad; it contains a kitchen, a dining-room, a bed-chamber, one small room, five closets for servants, and a cellar. The commissary's house (now occupied by officers) is built in the same line as this, its proportions and distribution of apartments are the same. Opposite these are the store-house and guard-house, they are each thirty yards long and eight broad; the former consists of two large store-rooms (under which is a large vaulted cellar) and a large room, a bed-chamber, and a closet for the store-keeper; the latter, of a soldier's and officer's guard-room, a chapel, a bed-chamber and closet for the chaplain, and artillery store-room. The lines of barracks have never been finished; they at present consist of two rooms each, for officers, and three rooms for soldiers; they are good spacious rooms of twenty-two feet square, and have betwixt them a small passage. There are fine spacious lofts over each building which reach from end to end; these are made use of to lodge regimental stores, working and intrenching tools, &c. It is generally allowed that this is the most commodious and best built fort in North America.

In June 1764, following the end of the war, its commandant and garrison evacuated the fort save for a detachment of 40 men. British troops finally arrived to take possession of the fort on October 10, 1765.

The last fort to be built in the Mississippi River Valley was Fort de L'Assomption, renamed Fort Massiac. It was anticipated that if the British took Fort Duquesne in the east, they or their Indian allies might navigate

East curtain wall of the third Fort de Chartres, built from 1753. This volumetric restoration by the State of Illinois made during the 20th century gives an excellent view of the fort's walls and a good idea of the buildings within. It was the only French fort made of stone in the Mississippi Valley.

westward to the Mississippi. A fort was needed to act as a sentinel and so Fort de L'Assomption was built upon a bluff situated on the north bank of the Ohio River, 38 miles (61km) from its confluence with the Mississippi (near Metropolis, Illinois). Completed on June 20, 1757, the fort was built on a square plan with four large corner bastions. Its walls were "made of two rows of stockaded tree trunks, joined together … planted in the earth … with a banquette along the interior two feet high, for firing through loopholes … at a height of six feet in the outer wall; and with raised platforms at the flanked angles of the bastions for placing the guerrittes and some canons en barbette" (C13A, 40). The garrison consisted of about 110 soldiers and militiamen with perhaps 50 allied Indians. It was attacked in the late fall of 1757 by a large group of Cherokee Indians who were repulsed, the only hostile action against the fort. However, enemy Indians lurked nearby and were likely the cause of the loss of several soldiers and militiamen, especially in 1758. In 1759–60, Illinois commandant Macarty had the fort strengthened by having the wall "terraced, fraized and fortified… [with] piece on piece [timber], with a good ditch" (C11A, 105) so that it could resist artillery fire. It was also renamed Massiac in 1759 to honor the marquis of Massiac, then the current minister of the French Navy, but the fort's name became corrupted to "Massac" after the French regime. In 1763, its French garrison evacuated the fort and a band of Chickasaw Indians burned it down so that when British troops arrived, all they found were charred ruins. In 1794, the American army built another Fort Massac within the perimeter of the destroyed French fort.

FORTS OF THE LOWER MISSISSIPPI VALLEY

Fort Prudhomme (near Randolph, Tennessee) was built in 1682 by La Salle during his exploration of the Mississippi River. It was the first structure built by Europeans in the present state of Tennessee and was named after Pierre Prudhomme, the armorer of La Salle's expedition. After Prudhomme failed to return from a hunting trip, La Salle had the fort built for temporary protection. Prudhomme was found and La Salle left him in charge of the post while he traveled to the Gulf coast. On his return trip, he fell ill and spent 40 days recuperating at the fort before going on. The fort was then abandoned.

Fort Arkansas or Arkansas Post was established in 1686 by Henri De Tonti (probably at what is now called the Menard Site, Little Prairie, Arkansas). It was a small post that may have been occupied for only part of the year and it was abandoned in about 1699. In 1722, a small settlement was established (also at Little Prairie) and Lieutenant La Boulaye and 17 soldiers were posted there for two years and then withdrawn. The fort consisted of a small stockade that enclosed four of five buildings. In late 1731, a small garrison of a dozen men was again posted at Fort Arkansas. By 1734, the post had no stockade, none being deemed necessary, and consisted of a building 32ft long by 18ft wide (9.8m long by 5.5m wide) divided into three rooms, a small powder magazine, and a "barrack." Only the barrack had defensive features, consisting of loopholes for muskets and a stone wall surrounding it (C13A, 18). In 1738–39, a strong force of soldiers was posted to the area and built a stockade fort on a square plan with bastions that was used as a base during a campaign against the Chickasaw Indians. Years later, in May 1749, when all was quiet and the fort had only a dozen soldiers, a band of about 150 Chickasaws attacked and captured six men and women

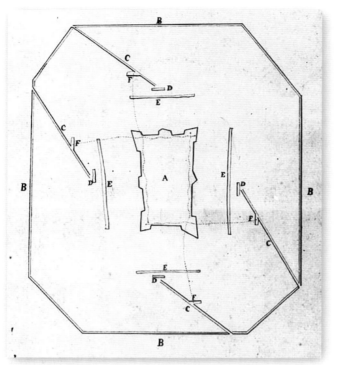

and children outside the fort, but abandoned their siege when their chief was killed by a cannonball. The fort was then relocated, probably between May and September 1749, at "Écores Rouges" or Red Bluffs, the site of the present Arkansas Post National Memorial. In 1751, its tiny garrison of a corporal and six men mutinied, sacked the storehouse and deserted to Spanish Texas. Governor Vaudreuil replaced them with a company of 50 men under Lieutenant de La Houssaye. Osage Indians raided the place in 1752, but were repulsed. In 1756, the fort was moved again and rebuilt downriver to a place about 10 miles (16km) from the mouth of the Arkansas (at an unknown site in present-day Desha County, Arkansas). It was occasionally called Fort Desha. That summer, the garrison was doubled to over 100 men, thereafter reduced to about 50 men in the following years until the end of the French regime. Pittman described the fort as being:

situated three leagues up the river Arcansas [sic], and is built with stockades, in a quadrangular form; the sides of the exterior polygon are about one hundred and eighty feet, and one three-pounder is mounted in the flanks and faces of each bastion. The buildings within the fort are, a barrack with three rooms for the soldiers, commanding officer's house, a powder magazine, and a magazine for provision, and an apartment for the commissary, all of which are in a ruinous condition. The fort stands about two hundred yards from the water-side, and is garrisoned by a captain, a lieutenant, and thirty French

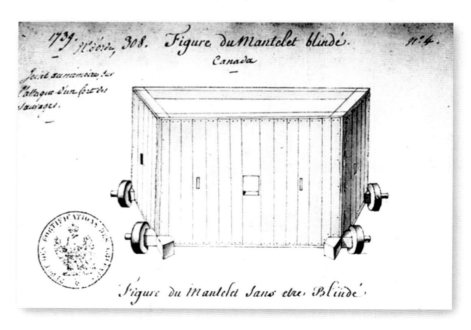

soldiers, including sergeants and corporals. There are eight houses without the fort, occupied by many families…

From 1769, a Spanish garrison replaced the French and ten years later, Arkansas Post was moved back to Red Bluffs.

Fort Saint-Jean-Baptiste des Natchitoches, more simply called Fort Natchitoches, was established on the shores of the Red River in 1714–15 (Natchitoches, Louisiana). Its purpose was to mark the western frontier of French Louisiana with that of New Spain and to promote alliances and trade with the area's Caddo Indians. The initial post built by Lieutenant Louis Juchereau de Saint-Denis with a detachment of soldiers consisted of a small storehouse and a lodging. In 1716, these buildings evolved into a fort that featured a stockade wall without bastions or artillery. Three years later, war was declared between France and Spain, and the French in Natchitoches raided and easily occupied the nearby Spanish mission of Los Adais and then withdrew. The Spanish came back in force and, in late 1721, built a presidio at Los Adais. The war soon ended and more settlers came to Natchitoches, so the fort was gradually extended. By 1733, it was laid out on a rectangular plan with small corner bastions with ten buildings inside including a church and a very long barrack block. Its ordnance consisted of two 4-pdr cannons, two 1-pdr cannons, and a swivel gun. In October 1731, Natchez Indians attacked

Fort Saint-Jean-Baptiste de Natchitoches in the 1730s. Founded in 1714, this post gradually grew into a thriving community. This reconstructed bird's-eye-view by New Orleans artist Auseklis Osols based on a 1733 plan gives a fine idea of what this medium-sized frontier fort surrounded by a protective stockade would have looked like. Based on this design, the modern town of Natchitoches, Louisiana, eventually had the fort reconstructed and it has since become an important site explaining the lives of the early settlers and soldiers. (Courtesy of Auseklis Osols and Koch and Wilson Architects, New Orleans)

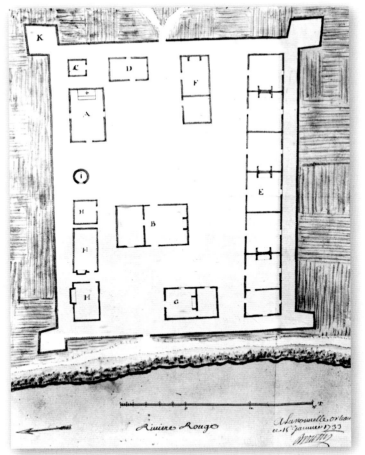

Natchitoches and were repulsed by its defenders, who consisted of 29 French regular soldiers, some 34 militiamen, about 250 allied Indian warriors, and a Spanish detachment of an officer and 16 men sent from Las Adais as reinforcements. The Natchez were said to have lost 74 warriors in their abortive attack. Because of recurrent floods, the old fort was abandoned and a new one built on higher ground. On November 7, 1767, the fort was turned over to the Spanish following the cession of all Louisiana territory west of the Mississippi to Spain.

Fort Rosalie (Natchez, Mississippi) was built from August 1716 on a height overlooking the east bank of the Mississippi River. The first fort was a rectangular stockade with four small bastions, added in 1719, and a few buildings within to lodge the commandant and the garrison according to Dumont de Montigny's 1721 memoir. A few settlements were established nearby. In 1729, Fort Rosalie was the scene of tragic events when, on November 28, the Natchez Indians staged a surprise attack on the fort, which was taken. Over 250 French settlers and soldiers were massacred, about 50 women and children and some 300 African slaves were kept as prisoners. Only one soldier escaped. The effect of Fort Rosalie's fall was considerable in the colony, which had a population of only 4,000 souls, nearly half of whom were slaves. Many French settlers feared a general Indian uprising. Things were not made easier when, shortly thereafter, a slave revolt plot was uncovered.

In New Orleans, Governor Perrier mobilized what regular forces he could muster and called out the militia and allied Indians. He also sent urgent messages to France and to Haiti asking for reinforcements. Ringleaders of the projected slave revolt were rounded up and executed and a military force of some 500 men was organized to campaign against the Natchez Indians. In January 1730, the French were joined by about 700 allied Choctaw and Tunica warriors and arrived in the area of Fort Rosalie. The outnumbered Natchez in the captured fort and fortified villages tried to resist. They were doomed when the French set up artillery batteries, and the Natchez surrendered. The French prisoners were freed, the Natchez women and children were given as slaves to the settlers and six warriors were burnt alive as retribution. Many Natchez managed to escape into the interior, but were tracked down by the French in January 1731, some 450 being captured and sent to the West Indies to be sold into slavery. However, around 250 warriors escaped and some joined the Chickasaw Indians who were also hostile to the French. Nevertheless, it was a strong signal to Indian nations that such

Fort Saint-Jean-Baptiste de Natchitoches, 1733. In January 1733, Engineer Ignace-François Broutin made this plan of it. Its rotting stockade had just been replaced by new "heavy stakes, nine feet high above ground, and doubled on the inside with other [stakes] six foot high above ground." Within were a church made of posts in the ground filled with mud between the joints (A), the commandant's house of timber frame filled with earth (B), a powder magazine of the same construction (C), a storehouse built like the church (D), barracks also of posts in the ground (E), lodging for the storekeeper (G), huts for the servants and slaves (H), and a bakery (I). (Archives Nationales [Aix-en-Provence, France], Dépot des Fortifications des Colonies, Louisiana)

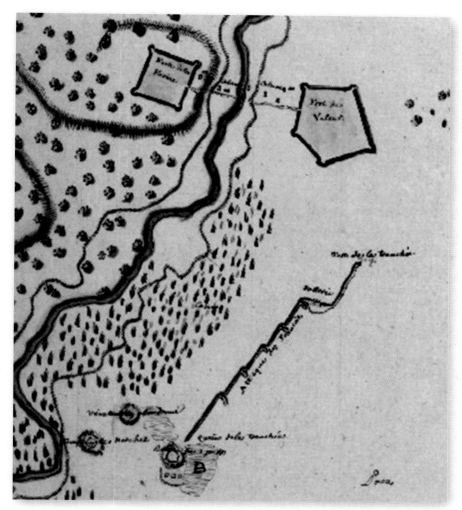

TOP

Detail from a plan showing the February 1730 siege by the French of two forts built by the Natchez Indians. These forts imitated the layout of French frontier forts with curtain walls and corner turrets. The French had to dig trenches and build a gun battery to overcome these fortifications. (Archives Nationales [Aix-en-Provence, France], Dépôt des Fortifications des Colonies, Louisiane)

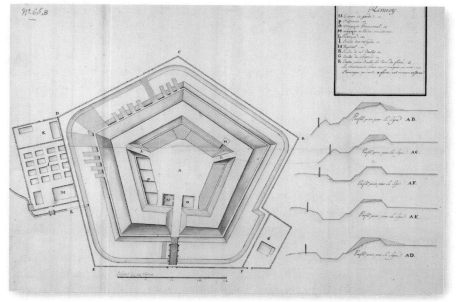

BOTTOM

Plan of Fort Rosalie or Natchez under construction, c.1732. The new fort replacing the one taken by the Indians in 1729 was a pentagon designed to be a substantial redoubt. Its five curtain walls had somewhat different profiles, which are shown at right. Inside the fort were the barracks (P), the guardhouse (N), the underground powder magazine (M), and the storehouse (O). Outside were various structures such as the hospital (H) and the blacksmith's shop (G). The features shaded in yellow were not completed when the plan was made. When he saw the fort in August 1764, Philip Pittman noted that these "buildings are made of framed timber, filled up with mud and *barbe espagnole*, (a kind of moss, which grows in great abundance on all the trees in Louisiana), and in this country that manner of building houses is very common. The *barbe espagnole* (which resembles a black curly beard) is also made use of for stuffing mattresses." (Archives Nationales [Aix-en-Provence, France], Dépôt des Fortifications des Colonies, Louisiane)

49

behavior would be strongly repressed. Meanwhile, a new Fort Rosalie was built on the site of the first fort. It was radically different from the former picket fort, being a large earthwork pentagon-shaped redoubt designed by Assistant Major de Bessan, who was familiar with engineering. This fort, which was much stronger and could withstand an enemy armed with artillery, had no substantial changes thereafter. It was renamed Fort Panmure when taken over by the British in 1763.

Fort Saint-Pierre or "Les Yazoos" was built in 1719 on the bluffs on the east side of the Yazoo River (10 miles or 16km north of Vicksburg, Mississippi). Dumont de Montigny mentions that it was merely a square stockade. Its garrison consisted of 48 men in August 1721 (Guerre, A1, 2592). In January 1722, a company of soldiers with some workmen was sent there to build a new fort laid out on a 180ft^2 (18m^2) plan with bastions, each bastion's side having two embrasures for its four cannons, with a guardhouse and lodgings for officers and men inside. It had a moat 12ft (3.7m) wide, so its main gate had a drawbridge. From about 1725, it had a garrison of an officer and 15 men (B, 43). In early December 1729, it was taken by surprise by a group of Natchez Indians who, pretending to be on a peaceful visit, were soon "knocking all its garrison on the head" according to Le Page du Pratz. The site was abandoned thereafter.

Fort Saint-François was built in the summer of 1739 as a supply depot on the west bank of the Mississippi River at the mouth of the St Francis River (near Helena, Arkansas) for the army setting out against the Chickasaw Indians. It had storehouses, barracks, and quarters for Governor Bienville. Following the end of the campaign in April 1740, Governor Bienville "caused Fort St Francis to be demolished, as it was now become useless" (Le Page du Pratz).

Fort de L'Assomption (on the Margot River near the east end of the Mississippi bridge at Memphis, Tennessee) was another temporary fortified base of operations and storage depot built in 1739, shortly after Fort Saint-François (see above), by the French force campaigning against the Chickasaw Indians. Governor Bienville wished to have such a base close to the territory of the Chickasaws. The fort's construction was begun on the day commemorating the Virgin Mary's assumption to heaven and was named in honor of this event. Like Fort Saint-François, its stockade enclosed storehouses, barracks, and quarters for Governor Bienville. It was dismantled in 1740, following the peace treaty signed with the Indian nations. In 1757, another Fort de L'Assomption, later renamed Fort Massiac, was built in Illinois (see above).

Following some raids by Choctaw Indians in 1748, the village of the "Côte des Allemands" (or German Coast) had a detachment of troops posted in "a small stockaded fort in the middle of the settlement on the east side of the [Mississippi] river" (Pittman). It consisted of a square palisade 102ft (31.11m) per side. The main building inside was 44.6ft long (13.6m) by 9.6ft wide (3m) and built of beams with a straw-mixture fill (C13A, 46).

The Tunicas or "Tonikas" referred to an Indian nation allied to the French settled on the banks of the lower Mississippi Valley. In 1715, Governor Bienville had a stockade fort built at the Tunicas with lodging for officers and troops. It seems to have been later abandoned. A permanent detachment of troops was stationed there in a small stockade fort from about 1751 (VP, 94).

Fort Pointe Coupé was built on the right bank of the Mississippi River above Baton Rouge. A company was posted there from about 1751 (VP, 94). According to Pittman, it consisted of "a quadrangle with four bastions, is built with stockades, and contains a very handsome house for the commanding officer, good barracks for the soldiers, store-houses and a prison."

THE GULF COAST AND THE "ALIBAMONS"

Fort Saint-Louis (Inez, Texas) was the setting for some of the most tragic events in French overseas history. Following his discovery in 1682 that the Mississippi River flowed into the Gulf of Mexico. Cavelier de La Salle obtained Louis XIV's blessing to lead an expedition from France to establish a settlement at the mouth of the Mississippi River. Through a combination of imprecise maps, faulty bearings, and strong currents, the three ships did not find the Mississippi River and landed instead at Matagorda Bay, on the coast of Texas, in early 1685. One of the ships, *L'Aimable*, was wrecked there. Some 180 colonists, including several women and children, soldiers, and sailors landed on February 20, 1685. They built a fort out of timbers salvaged from the ship and armed it with its eight iron naval cannons. It featured a large timber building, built "in the Canadian manner" according to Henri Joutel, roofed with boards and raw hides, and divided into four apartments, three for lodging La Salle, the Recollet priests, and the officers while the fourth was a storeroom. According to a sketch later made by the Spanish, a chapel and several smaller buildings were added and enclosed by a rectangular palisade. One of the remaining ships, *Le Joly*, went back to France while the other, *La Belle*, remained in Texas but was wrecked in 1686. The 180 settlers, soldiers and sailors were plagued by disease and suffered from malnutrition; only about 45 remained by January 1687. La Salle led several small, unsuccessful search parties in repeated attempts to locate the Mississippi and was finally assassinated in the spring of 1687 by one of his own disgruntled men. There were also skirmishes with hostile Karankawa Indians. The 20 remaining colonists at the fort survived until late 1688 or early 1689 when the Karankawa Indians attacked. All were killed except for five French children who were taken captive. Having heard of La Salle's expedition landing on the coast of Texas, the Viceroy of New Spain sent a military force to locate it and assert Spain's territorial dominion. When the Spanish soldiers reached the area in April 1689, they found a fort in ruins and the remains of three of the French settlers. They gave the dead settlers a proper burial and burned what remained of Fort Saint-Louis. The Spanish troops also buried the eight French cannons they found in the fort. The Spanish eventually established their own fort at the site of Fort Saint-Louis in 1722 but never relocated the cannons. They were found and excavated by archeologists in 1996.

Plan and elevation of Fort Biloxi (or Fort Maurepas) at Biloxi, 1699. The fort was armed with at least a dozen cannons. A: parade; B: Royal Bastion; C: Biloxi Bastion; D: Chapel Bastion; E: Sea Bastion; F: governor's quarters; G: major's quarters; H and I: platforms; K: storehouse; L: powder magazine; M: quarters for the Canadians and freebooters; N: soldiers' barracks; O: well; P: oven; Q: chapel; R: covered way; S: curtain; T: Royal Gate; V: drainage canal. This fort was abandoned in the spring of 1702. (Library and Archives Canada, NMC29193)

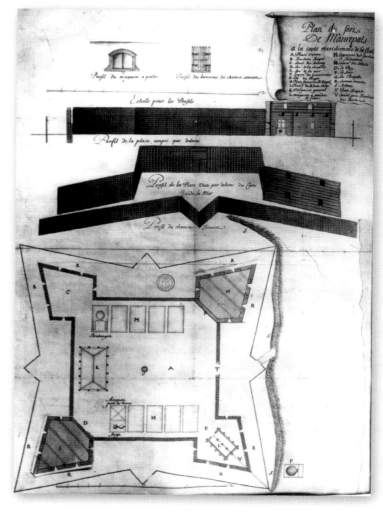

Fort Biloxi or Maurepas at Biloxi, 1699

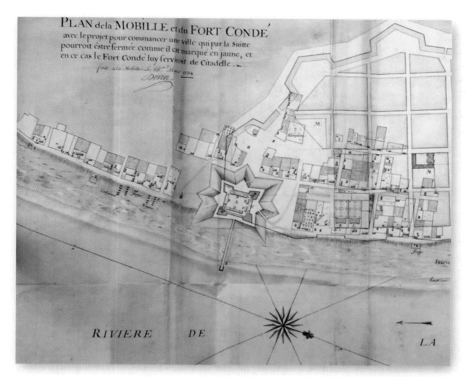

Part of a plan of the town of Mobile with Fort Condé at its center, 1734. The fortifications and city blocks outlined in orange at the upper right were suggested, but were never built. During the next thirty years, there were hardly any changes to the fort. (Archives Nationales [Aix-en-Provence, France], Dépôt des Fortifications des Colonies, Louisiane)

Fort Biloxi, also called Fort Maurepas, was the first permanent French establishment in Lower Louisiana (now Ocean Springs, Mississippi) and led to the settlement of other areas on the Gulf Coast. It was built in Biloxi Bay by Pierre Le Moyne d'Iberville and his men who completed it on May 1, 1699. It consisted of a timber fort with four bastions mounted with artillery. The site, however, proved unhealthy and inconvenient so that, in 1702, the garrison moved east to build Fort Louis at the entrance of Mobile Bay. In 1720, detachments were again posted at "Old Biloxi" and another "fort" that may have been simply a battery was constructed at Ile aux Vaisseaux (Ship Island) south of Biloxi Bay (C13A, 6). In 1721, plans were made following a proposal to build a new and larger settlement with a substantial fort that was intended to become the colonial capital across the bay from the "Old Biloxi" fort. Some work started on this "New Biloxi" project, but various difficulties soon arose and, the following year, New Orleans became the effective capital of Louisiana. The Biloxi garrisons were withdrawn sometime after October 1723.

The first fort at Mobile was named Fort Louis and constructed in 1702 on the shore of Mobile Bay. It consisted of four semi-circular bastions mounted with artillery and connected by a palisade. Within were several buildings

E   FORT BILOXI OR MAUREPAS AT BILOXI, 1699

Although often called Biloxi, this fort was officially named after Louis Phélypeaux de Pontchartrain, count of Maurepas (1643–1727) who was French minister of the Navy at the time Captain Pierre Le Moyne d'Iberville had the fort built in the spring of 1699. Made of wood on a square plan with four large bastions, the fort was armed with at least a dozen cannons. It featured a chapel, quarters for the officers (the governor having the largest

building), much smaller lodgings for Canadians, freebooters, and soldiers; a storehouse, a powder magazine, a well, and an oven. Outside were a covered way and a drainage canal. The curtain walls and two bastions were made of logs planted in the ground. The two other bastions were of timber laid horizontally and had an upper-level floor. This fort was abandoned in the spring of 1702 when its garrison moved to Fort Louis on Mobile Bay.

including a guardhouse and the officers' quarters. Barracks were built later and outside the fort. Because of frequent flooding, this fort was abandoned in 1710 and another was built farther south on the bay, where the cannons were remounted and all "supplies and furniture" were moved (Margry, V). Commandant La Mothe Cadillac described it in October 1713 as having had a cedar log stockade with four small bastions. It was about 576 English feet (175m) from bastion tip to bastion tip according to archeological surveys. Inside were the governor's quarters, a guardhouse, and a storehouse. The guns were "near the water" and possibly mounted in a temporary waterfront battery (C13A, 3). Obviously, a more permanent and solid structure was needed and, during 1717, work started on a new fort made of brick and stone built on a square plan with bastions. Its brick walls laid on a sandstone foundation were 20 English feet (6m) high. It was a smaller fort, being approximately 360 English feet (110m) from bastion tip to bastion tip, and was surrounded by a dry moat and a glacis. The main gate was through the north curtain wall. In 1724, it was renamed Fort Condé after the great general of the 17th century. This fortification, which featured casemates in three of its four curtain walls, was meant to resist a European enemy arriving by land or sea and it was certainly the strongest work on the French Gulf Coast. In time, the town grew around the fort. During the War of Austrian Succession, it was feared that hostile Chickasaw and Muscigee Indians might stage raids so, in 1747, a wooden palisade enclosed the town. Fort Condé always had a large garrison since it was the seat of the "Lieutenant du Roi" (lieutenant-governor) of Louisiana. The garrison consisted of several companies of Compagnies Franches de la Marine with a strong detachment of the Karrer (Halwyll from

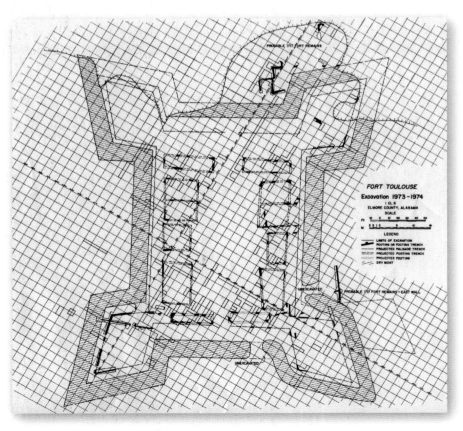

Fort Toulouse (Alabama), 1973–74 excavation plan. The outline of the four bastions and the connecting curtain walls are clearly visible within the surrounding dry moat. The foundations of ten buildings within the fort were discovered. At lower right are the probable remains of a bastion associated with the first fort built on the site in 1717. (Courtesy of Donald Heldman)

ABOVE
A squad of soldiers at Fort de Chartres repair a garrison carriage before remounting its cannon, c.1755. The larger forts, even on the frontier, could have fairly heavy artillery besides the usual swivel guns. The types of ordnance were mainly French Navy iron guns mounted on garrison carriages. (Model at the Fort de Chartres Museum)

LEFT
Fort Crèvecoeur was built in January 1680 by Robert Cavelier de La Salle and his men in the area of present-day Peoria, Illinois, to protect the Ilini [Illinois] Indian nation from their Iroquois enemies. It was abandoned in April 1680. (Print after R. Smart illustrating Arthur Lagron's reconstruction from La Salle's description)

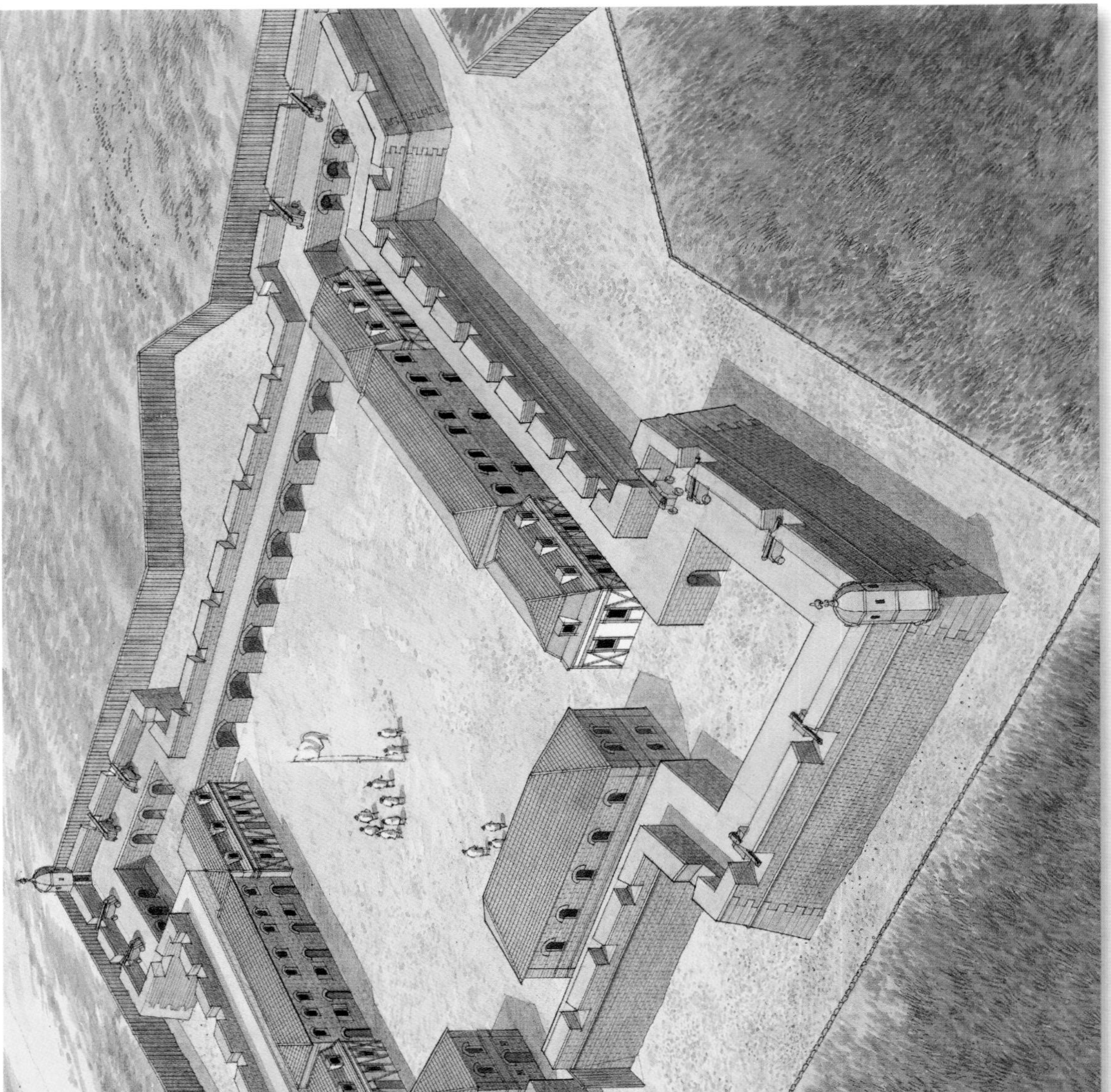

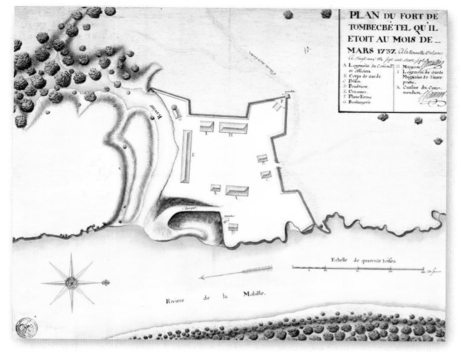

Fort Tombecbé, March of 1737. In April 1736, a small picket fort was first built on the bluff above the river by the French army on campaign against the Chickasaw Indians. The French Army's tent camp was outside this first small fort. It was later decided to maintain a permanent military post at that site, and a much larger fortified enclosure was designed and built. Engineer Broutin's plan of the fort "as it was in March 1737" shows that he took full advantage of the bluff and rivers, putting the buildings on high ground and building a bastioned wall on the landward sides. The long building at left is the soldiers' barracks, with the storehouse at the upper right, officers' quarters at the lower right, the powder magazine below, the guardhouse and jail near the gate, and the bakery in the upper left half-bastion. (Archives Nationales [Aix-en-Provence, France], Dépôt des Fortifications des Colonies, Louisiane)

1752) Swiss Regiment and, from 1744, an artillery school. On October 20, 1763, a British detachment arrived to relieve the French garrison. Fort Condé was renamed Fort Charlotte, in honor of King George III's wife.

Fort de la Boulaye (about a mile north of Phoenix, Louisiana, near the Gulf of Mexico) was the first French post in the present state of Louisiana. It was built in February 1700 by a party of soldiers led by Pierre Le Moyne d'Iberville on a low ridge along the east bank of the Mississippi River. It consisted of a 28ft^2 (3m^2) wooden blockhouse armed with six cannons and had a garrison of 18 men to secure France's claim to the mouth of the Mississippi River. It was abandoned in 1707. For the later forts, such as La Balise, leading to New Orleans, see Fortress 27: *French Fortresses in North America 1535–1763*, René Chartrand (Osprey: Oxford, 2005).

Dauphine Island, near the entrance to Mobile Bay, had its first settlers during the early 18th century. In 1709, a fort with embrasures for its cannons was built there although this may have been more of a coastal battery. A church was also built at the same time. Seven years later, a fort was built near the shore. However, from Dumont de Montigny's 1719 plan of the island, it

F   FORT CONDÉ AT MOBILE

The most important French fort on the Gulf Coast was Fort Condé built from 1717 to defend Mobile (now in the US state of Alabama). It was conceived to resist a European enemy attacking by land or by sea. It was an impressive-looking structure that was "magnificent, made all of bricks, [with] four bastions and well fortified" according to Dumont de Montigny. The moat was some 23ft (7m) wide. The 7ft-wide (2.1m) wall foundations were of ferruginous sandstone rock upon which large flat bricks of an orange hue were laid. The mortar was of crushed oysters, clam shells, lime, and sand. Built inside were

eight vaulted casemates along the south and east walls and seven vaulted casemates at the north wall. The west wall simply had buttresses behind the soldier's barracks. The fort had a substantial number of iron navy guns mounted on its walls, and from the 1740s Fort Condé was the home of an artillery school. Each Louisiana infantry company had a few soldiers trained to serve guns and, from 1759–60, a regular company of artillery was organized. Fort Condé was never attacked during the French regime, but in 1780 the Spanish took it from the British after a week's siege.

appears that this new fort may in fact have been two additional batteries. Spanish ships attacked the island in May 1719, but were repulsed by its coastal batteries. In the 1720s the island's importance waned owing to its ship's channel being filled with sand, and its small garrison was eventually withdrawn.

Fort Toulouse was built in 1717 on a bluff at the junction of the Coosa and Tallapoosa rivers (near Wetumpka and Montgomery, Alabama). It was also called "Les Alibamons" because the Alibamon (or Alabama) Indians, a branch of the Creek Indian nation, resided nearby. The fort was meant to foster trade and alliances with the Indians, and guard Louisiana's eastern frontier against incursions by the Anglo-Americans from the Carolinas and the Spanish in Florida. It was a stockade fort built on a square plan with four bastions. Its soil and location was not ideal and the fort was threatened with erosion. In 1721, repairs were required and, in 1736, the stockade was rebuilt with oak logs. As time passed, flooding and the crumbling riverbank dictated that the fort should be moved back and reconstructed. This was done in 1751 under the guidance of Captain Francois Saucier. According to archeological surveys made in the early 1970s, the second fort was built close to the original fort and had a slightly rectangular plan, its stockade walls being about 60m by 45m, each corner having a bastion containing one or two guns. A watchtower overlooked the north wall onto the Coosa River. A dry moat surrounded the whole fort. There may have been up to ten frame-buildings within. Fort Toulouse was never attacked. Initially, the garrison lived in appalling conditions and, in 1722, some 24 soldiers mutinied and locked up the officers. The officers escaped and, with the help of the nearby Creek Indians, pursued and killed 16 of the mutineer soldiers and captured the others who were turned over to the authorities in Mobile. Thereafter, the garrison's conditions obviously improved and many soldiers settled on farms near the fort. Following the cession of eastern Louisiana to Great Britain in 1763, the fort was evacuated but was not occupied by British troops.

In 1717, an outpost named Fort Crèvecoeur was built on the east shore of St Joseph's Bay (Florida) to keep an eye on the Spanish in nearby Pensacola. It was abandoned in early 1718.

According to Dumont de Montigny, the first Fort Tombecbé was built by a detachment of troops sent up the Mobile River in August 1735. It consisted of a small, square, picketed fort with four bastions built on the bluff above the river's west bank where it meets with a small river. In April 1736, a French force on campaign against the Chickasaw Indians (about 650 troops and militia with African slaves as laborers) set up its tent camp outside the fort. It was decided to enlarge and rebuild the fortifications for a permanent military post situated at that site. By March 1737, a much larger fort had been built. Until the early 1760s, about 25 men detached from Mobile who stood guard under a commandant that was "senior and experienced as Choctaw [Indians] merit attention" were posted there, although the fort was said to lack housing in 1751 (VP, 94).

THE FORTS TODAY

To travel to all of the fort sites mentioned in this book would be next to impossible. Most can be reached by using the Interstate Highway system in the United States and its equivalent in Canada, which leads to many secondary roads, or even dirt roads. Once on the spot, the visitor experience varies greatly. In places such as Fort Niagara, Fort de Chartres, or Fort Condé, one is presented with remarkably good preservation and/or reconstructions. For instance, the "French Castle" at Fort Niagara remains today one of the best-preserved and most impressive original buildings on the frontier. Such sites have museums, interpretive staff on the site, and often hold special events of great interest. However, to see Fort Frontenac, one must settle for a few stones in the middle of a military parking lot in Kingston (Ontario), while the real site of Fort Ouiatenon is in the middle of a farmer's field near Lafayette (Indiana) with no site marker (as of 2008). Many other sites have simply vanished under skyscraper cities, such as the forts in Toronto, Chicago, or Detroit, or were claimed by nature. The material used to make frontier forts (wood) was not meant to last. Be that as it may, many of these now-vanished historic forts are the basis for today's vibrant communities, large and small, which makes traveling to these sites a very pleasant and fulfilling exploration.

GLOSSARY OF FORTIFICATION TERMS

Abbatis
A defensive barricade or row of obstructions made up of closely-spaced felled trees, their tops toward the enemy, their branches trimmed to points and interlaced where possible.

Banquette
A continuous step or ledge at the interior base of a parapet on which defenders stood to direct musket fire over the top of the wall. A fire step.

Bastion
A projection in the enceinte, made up of four sides, two faces and two flanks, which better enabled a garrison to defend the ground adjacent to the main or curtain walls.

Barbette
Said of cannons placed over a rampart without the protective embrasures.

Battery
An emplacement for artillery.

Berm
A line of wooden stakes or logs, 6–8ft (1.8–2.4m) long, planted in the middle of a ditch and pointing vertically.

Breastwork
See Parapet.

Casemate
A mortar-bomb or shell-proof chamber located within the walls of defensive works; generally pierced with openings for weapons; loopholes for muskets or embrasures for cannon.

Cordon
The coping or top course of a scarp or a rampart, sometimes of different-colored stone and set proud from the rest of the wall. The point where a rampart stops and a parapet begins.

Counterguard
Defensive work built in a ditch in front of a bastion to give it better protection.

Covered way
A depression, road or path in the outer edge of a fort's moat or ditch, generally protected from enemy fire by a parapet,

at the foot of which might be a banquette enabling the coverage of the glacis with musketry.

Cunette	A furrow located in the bottom of a dry ditch for the purpose of drainage.
Curtain	The wall of a fort between two bastions.
Demi-bastion	A half-bastion with only one face and one flank.
Demi-lune	Triangular-shaped defensive work built in a ditch in front of a bastion or of a curtain wall.
Ditch	A wide, deep trench around a defensive work. When filled with water it was termed a moat or wet ditch; otherwise a dry ditch, or fosse.
Embrasure	An opening in a wall or parapet allowing cannon to fire through it, the gunners remaining under cover. The sides of the embrasure were called "cheeks," the bottom called the "sole," the narrow part of the opening called the "throat," and the wide part called the "splay."
En barbette	An arrangement for cannon to be fired directly over the top of a low wall instead of through embrasures.
Enfilade fire	Fire directed from the flank or side of a body of troops, or along the length of a ditch, parapet, or wall. Guns in the flank of a bastion can direct enfilade fire along the face of the curtain.
Epaulement	A parapet or work protecting against enfilade fire.
Fascines	Long bundles of sticks or small-diameter tree branches bound together for use in revetments, for stabilizing earthworks, filling ditches, etc.
Fosse or foss	*See* Ditch.
Fraise	A defense of closely placed stakes or logs, 6–8ft (1.8–2.4m) long, driven or dug into the ground and sharpened; arranged to point horizontally or obliquely outward from a defensive position.
Gabion	A large, round, woven wicker cylinder intended to be set in place and filled with earth, sand, or stones.
Gallery	An interior passageway or corridor that ran along the base of a fort's walls.
Gate	A main entrance to a fortress.
Glacis	A broad, gently sloped earthwork or natural slope in front of a fort, separated from the fort proper by a ditch and outworks and so arranged as to be swept with musket or cannon fire.

Gorge	The interval or space between the two curtain angles of a bastion. In a ravelin, the area formed by the flanked angle and either left open or enclosed.
Guardhouse	The headquarters for the daily guard.
Guérite	A small lookout watchtower, usually located on the upper outer corner of a bastion.
Half-bastion	*See* Demi-bastion.
Hornwork	A work made up of a bastion front; two half-bastions and a curtain and two long sides termed branches.
Loopholes	Small openings in walls or stockades through which muskets were fired.
Machicoulis	Projections in old castles and over gates, left open above to throw stones, etc. on enemies below. These were built into several forts in Canada.
Magazine	A place for the storage of gunpowder, arms, or goods generally related to ordnance.
Merlon	The solid feature between embrasures in a parapet.
Moat	*See* Ditch.
Orgue	*See* Portcullis.
Outwork	An outer defense, inside the glacis but outside the body of the place. A ravelin is an outwork.
Palisade	A high fence made of stakes, poles, palings, or pickets, supported by rails and set endwise in the ground 6–9in. apart. *See* Stockade.

Parapet	A breastwork or protective wall over which defenders, standing on banquettes, fired their weapons.
Portcullis	A timber or iron grating that can be lowered to close the gates of a fortress. Called "*orgue*" (organ) in French.
Postern	A passage leading from the interior of a fortification to the ditch.
Rampart	The mass of earth, usually faced with masonry, formed to protect an enclosed area.
Ravelin	An outwork consisting of two faces forming a salient angle at the front and a flank angle to the rear that was usually closed at the gorge. Ravelins were separated from the main body of the place by ditches and functioned to protect curtains.
Redoubt	An enclosed fortification without bastions.
Revetment	The sloping wall of stone or brick supporting the outer face of a rampart.
Sallyport	A passageway within the rampart, usually vaulted, leading from the interior of a fort to the exterior, primarily to provide for sorties.
Sap	A trench and parapet constructed by besiegers to protect their approaches toward a fortification.
Scarp	The interior side of a ditch or the outer slope of a rampart.
Stockade	A line or enclosure of logs or stakes set upright in the earth with no separation between them, to form a barrier 8ft (2.4m) or more high. Stockades were generally provided with loopholes. The loopholes were reached by banquettes or elevated walks. *See* Palisade.
Traverse	A parapet or wall thrown across a covered way, a terreplein, ditch, or other location to prevent enfilade or reverse fire along a work.

SELECT BIBLIOGRAPHY

Archives:
Archives Nationales (Aix-en-Provence, France), Colonies, series B, C11A, C13A,
        Dépôt des Fortifications des Colonies
Service Historique des Armées (Vincennes, France), series Guerre A1, maps and plans
Library and Archives Canada (Ottawa, Canada), maps and plans
Library of Congress (Washington DC, USA), maps and plans
The National Archives (Kew, UK), War Office (WO) 34 series, maps and plans

Publications:
Balvay, Arnaud, *L'Épée et la Plume*, Les presses de l'Université Laval: Québec (2006)
Barron, Bill, *The Vaudreuil Papers*, Polyanthos: New Orleans (1975). Cited as VP

Beaudouin, Marie-Noëlle, "Forts et postes de commerce de la Nouvelle-France", PhD thesis, École des Chartres: Paris (1964)

Bodin, Jacques, *L'histoire extraordinaire des soldats de la Nouvelle-France*, O.C.A. Communications: n.p. (1993)

Bougainville, Louis-Antoine de, *Écrits sur le Canada*, Septentrion: Sillery (1993), pp. 72–111

Brown, Margaret Kimball and Dean, Lawrie Cena, *The French Colony in the Mid-Mississippi Valley*, American Kestrel Books: Cabondale (1995)

Champagne, Antoine, *Les La Vérendrye et le poste de l'ouest*, Les presses de l'Université Laval: Québec (1968)

Combet, Denis, ed., *In Search of the Western Sea: Selected Journals of La Vérendrye*, Great Plains Publications and Les éditions du blé: Winnipeg (2001)

Edmunds, R. David and Puyser, Joseph L., *The Fox Wars*, University of Oklahoma Press: Norman (1993)

Ferris, Robert G., ed., *Explorers and Settlers*, National Park Service: Washington (1968)

Faribeault-Beauregard, Marthe, *La population des forts français d'Amérique (XVIIIe siècle)*, Éditions Bergeron: Montréal (1982)

Giraud, Marcel, *Histoire de la Louisiane française*, Presses universitaires de France: Paris (1953-1974), four vols

Dumont de Montigny, Jean-François-Benjamin, *Regards sur le monde atlantique 1717–1747*, Septentrion: Sillery (2008)

Dunnigan, Brian Leigh, *Frontier Metropolis: picturing early Detroit 1701–1838*, Wayne State University Press: Detroit (2001) and *Glorious Old Relic: The French castle and Old Fort Niagara*, Old Fort Niagara: Youngstown (1987).

Gorrell, James, "Lieut. James Gorrell's journal. Commencing at Detroit, September 8th, 1761, and ending at Montreal, August 13th, 1763." *Wisconsin Historical Collections*, vol. 1 (1855): 24–48

Heldman, Donald P., *Archaeological Investigations of Fort Toulouse: 1972–1973*, Alabama Historical Commission and US National Park Service: Washington (1973)

Hoffhaus, Charles E., "Fort de Cavagnial", *Kansas Historical Quarterly* (Winter, 1964)

Kidd, Kenneth E., *The Excavation of Sainte-Marie I*, University of Toronto: Toronto (1949)

Le Page du Pratz, Antoine Simon, *The History of Louisiana*, London (1774)

Litalien, Raymonde, Jean-François Palomino and Vaugeois, Denis, *La mesure d'un continent: Atlas historique de l'Amérique du Nord*, Septentrion: Sillery (2008)

Lugan, Bernard, *Histoire de la Louisiane française 1682–1804*, Perrin: Paris (1994)

Margry, Pierre, *Découvertes et établissements des Français dans l'ouest et le sud de l'Amérique septentrionale 1614–1754*, Maisonneuve: Paris (1876–1886), six vols

McDermot, John Francis, ed., *The French in the Mississipi Valley*, University of Illinois Press: Urbana (1965) and *Frenchmen and French Ways in the Mississippi Valley*, University of Illinois Press: Urbana (1969)

Noble, Virgil E., *Discovering Fort Ouiatenon: Its History and Archaeology*, Tippecanoe County Historical Association: Lafayette (c.1982)

Preston, Richard, and Lamontagne, Léopold, *Royal Fort Frontenac*, Champlain Society: Toronto (1958)

Winter, Fritz G. M., *Old Forts of Upper Canada*, University of Toronto: Toronto (c.1935)

INDEX

Figures in **bold** refer to illustrations.